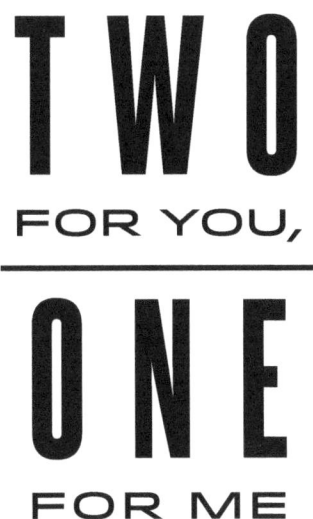

A mother and son wander aimlessly in the late 1920s through Arizona and Mexico border-town poverty, homeless, with no life direction; in the early 1930s her son discovers a better way to live through life's happenstance.

Anthony Hernández

Copyright © 2026 by Anthony Hernández
All rights reserved. No part of this publication may be reproduced, distributed, or transmitted in any form or by any means, including photocopying, recording, digital scanning, or other electronic or mechanical methods, without the prior written permission of the publisher, except in the case of brief quotations embodied in critical reviews and certain other noncommercial uses permitted by copyright law. For permission requests, please address the author at: 2foryou1formepublishing@gmail.com.

Second edition published by 2 for You, 1 for Me Publishing
Bothell, WA
Printed in the United States of America

ISBN:978-1-7321095-3-7 (Paperback)

DEDICATION

This book is dedicated, in part, to the memory of my father, mother, brother, and sister, and all that they each gave me over the years. My immediate family was my centerpiece as I grew up and helped to launch me into the wonderful life that awaited living. Also, to my father's extended family members, some of whom I only met during my research in Tucson, who were able to provide me their support as well as important family history and photographs unbeknownst to me when I started this effort. Additionally, in memory of the Mendoza family, to all of the freely given acts of kindness from strangers to those people in need, yesterday, today, and tomorrow, that can potentially alter the course of life for the giver and receiver. And lastly, and most significantly, to my wife, Patty, for all of her patience over the years with this endeavor, and her interest, assistance, and support in helping me with my odyssey to honor my commitment to finish and publish the memoir Dad so reluctantly started and completed for me and my siblings.

CONTENTS

SON'S PROLOGUE

ix

FATHER'S INTRODUCTION

xix

PART ONE

1927–1933

The Toughest Years – Two Insignificant People
Living Insignificant Lives

- 1 -

Vergara Family Photographs

- 46 -

Images of Cities and Towns Routinely Visited

- 51 -

PART TWO
1934–1936
The Mendoza Family – A New Beginning
- 61 -

PART THREE
April 1939 – September 1940
The Civilian Conservation Corps – Discipline, Responsibility, Manhood
- 81 -

PART FOUR
October 1940 – November 1941
An Army Life Takes Me Further from My Roots and Culture; Speaking English Is an Army Requirement
- 109 -

PART FIVE
December 1941 – March 1942
Attack on Pearl Harbor Changes Everything and the Course of My Life to Follow
- 141 -

PART SIX
April 1942–Spring 1944
A Blind Date Leads to Marriage and a Life That Grounds Me
- 161 -

Humphreys Family Photographs
- 183 -

My Father's Service Photographs
- 187 -

PART SEVEN
Summer 1944–November 1945
The Pacific War Intensifies and Overseas Duty Calls Me
- 191 -

PART EIGHT
December 1945–1952
A Homecoming to Remember; My Civilian Life Begins
- 221 -

PART NINE
1953–1975
More Good Memories; I Transition from Blue Collar to White Collar Employment; My Personal Life Choices of Family Consequence
- 259 -

Hernández Family Memories
- 283 -

SON'S EPILOGUE
- 295 -

SON'S PROLOGUE

Over the years while growing up in our family, given my inquisitive nature, I had more than an idle curiosity regarding my father's upbringing, his origins and roots, all of which he was careful to withhold. This was somewhat disappointing to me, especially in light of the fact that my dad seemed to have no parents while my mother's father lived with us at times, and, as told to me by my mother when I was old enough, her mother and newborn baby sibling both died as a result of a difficult childbirth when my grandmother was only thirty-nine years old.

As a youngster I would ask my mother about Dad, and she would tell me that his childhood was painful and he just didn't like to talk about it. As I grew to adolescence, when I inquired, Dad would dribble out information and, somewhat willingly, share incidental thoughts regarding certain family members and guarded recollections of his childhood. Even when we infrequently visited some of his extended family in San Jose, California, or especially in Mexicali and Calexico, Mexico, where my dad spoke mostly Spanish to those relatives, there was never any substantive information obtained beyond so-and-so is my uncle or aunt or cousin. So over the years this void continued.

Then, in my late forties in March of 1995 during one of our

somewhat frequent telephone visits together, the subject of Dad's life and my lack of knowledge of it were eagerly discussed on my part. I broached the subject of him writing his life story down on paper and I would edit it as he wrote, with the hope that my mother and brother and I would finally have Dad's history. I expressed to him that he might enjoy and have the satisfaction of leaving for us the legacy of his early life story, especially given my fateful reconnection with my biological son and his wife and children. My father welcomed the idea and committed to do it.

So, what started out for my father as a favor to me and other family members, soon became for him an emotional and unpleasant reliving of memories and experiences, some of which were quite painful and difficult to confront and share. For me it was an eye-opener, to say the least, as I lived and experienced my father's pain through his words put to paper. My disbelief and compassion were palpable as I carefully read his words and thoughtfully edited his early life stories, verifying with him as we proceeded. With patience and encouragement provided over some tearful telephone conversations, we talked through these emotional moments. Dad's effort eventually proved to be cathartic for him and he was able to complete this history of his formative years, and then proceeded up to the time when he and my mother divorced after thirty-three years of marriage. My Dad was fifty-three years old at the time of my parents' divorce.

My father was born in August of 1922 in Nogales, Arizona, and in December of that year, he was baptized Richard Edmundo Hernández in Douglas, Arizona, after his biological father, Edmundo Hernández. Unfortunately, my dad's father's life and the facts and circumstances of the ending of Edmundo's marriage to Dad's mother, Guadalupe, remained unknown throughout my father's life, and subsequently, my immediate family's lives. Those members of my dad's extended family possessing that information have long since passed, and if Dad did have any knowledge, he chose to take it with him to the grave. Of course, over the time period of our collaborative writing effort, I have quietly speculated that my grandmother's aimless wanderings were possibly driven by her need to continue to frequent the border towns in search of lost promises and dreams shared with her husband, Edmundo, either still living, having abandoned or divorced her, or deceased due to accident, illness, or worse. And, along the way, alcohol became Guadalupe's friend, confidant, and source of comfort.

My most recent research produced a documented, recorded Certificate of Marriage dated May 26, 1921, for Edmundo Hernández and Guadalupe Vergara, and subsequent shared addresses where they lived together in Douglas, Arizona, up to the mid-1920s, as found in Douglas phone books from those years. The discovery of the marriage certificate and addresses finally answered for me the mystery as to why and how the "random" baptism of my father occurred in Douglas, Arizona. What was known to me before my research was an unexplained, significant familial event, completely unconnected to the early years preceding Dad's memory and writings. Until now, only this memoir sets forth what my father remembered and/or chose to include in his recollections.

My father's early childhood years were made up of life's sometimes cruel and random events set in the poverty of the late 1920s and early 1930s Mexico and Arizona border towns. He experienced frequent separation and parental abandonment from his alcoholic mother who imposed a vagabond lifestyle, absent of consistent parental love and nurturing as well as formal schooling. These times were in contrast with the blessing of the kindness of individual strangers; the occasional comfort of a night's stay with a fellow child, another street hustler who happened to have a place to sleep, or better yet a home; and welcome but limited stays with extended family before Dad's mother took him in hand to wander once again for days, always to someplace else. Over time my father's childhood realities shaped his strength of character and drive to survive, and he became a survivor in the truest sense. Ultimately, in the mid-1930s the state of Arizona authorities intervened on my father's behalf and permanently reunited him with his grandparents and aunts and uncles living in Tucson.

In the end, for me, my lifetime of unknowing was replaced with a greater sense of my father's total being. My respect, appreciation, and understanding of him grew considerably as a result of his sharing personal life experiences with me. What difficulties and trying times he endured as a child are in such stark contrast to the kind of man, father, and husband he became during the important formative and adolescent years of his children's lives and his marriage to my mother.

Fortunately, Dad did live to finish his writing and read the unresearched, preliminary, edited draft of his life story. However, my brother and sister did not. Richard Jr. and Sherry Lynn both passed away from cancer much too early in life; my brother in 2001 at age fifty-seven, and my sister in 1990 at forty-five years old. My mother, Janet, passed away in 2005 at eighty years of age. Fortunately, both my mother and brother were able to read early drafts of what Dad had written up to that point in time, so they both knew this was an early work in progress.

Subsequently, over the years my father and I would tweak and add to his story as I continued periodically to edit his additions, questioning and verifying certain parts through discussions with him during our walks or telephone calls with one another. He knew and understood that my goal was to complete and self-publish for family and friends, and, if possible, a commercial effort to be undertaken in both

Son's Prologue

English and Spanish. In the end Dad was so pleased with himself and satisfied that he had fulfilled his commitment to complete his story with and for me. Though at the time my intent was to finish and publish it while he was still alive, it seems life got in my way to do so. With his passing on June 6, 2012, three months short of his ninetieth birthday, I recommitted to get this done through completion of some additional and necessary research that, in and of itself, increased and stretched my odyssey to complete this book.

That renewed effort took me to additional public archival research, both through the internet and by physically traveling to locations. I used some local government resources of city, county, and state libraries as well as those of the University of Washington in Seattle and University of Arizona in Tucson; a few local historical societies in the Puget Sound area and in Tucson and Douglas, Arizona; identification of known and unknown family historical information sources that were very helpful to me to verify dates uncertain or forgotten, as well as the chronological flow of certain life events; known family and unknown extended family photographs and my family's collection of eight millimeter home movies; national archival information from both the National Archives located in St. Louis for access to Civilian Conservation Corp records, and in Seattle on Sand Point Way for copies of my research results; immediate and extended family tree history and photographs revealed through Ancestry.com resources; and additional cassette tapes provided by my mother of some of her relevant early, adolescent, and later lifetime memories.

Lastly, my research efforts benefited greatly from two other significant sources that proved to be invaluable and must be mentioned separately. The *first* was one of the prize possessions of my mother's marriage to my father: all of the 248 marvelously handwritten letters that Dad wrote to her, and some of those she wrote to him, during World War II, from 1942 up to his coming home for Christmas in 1945 from the war in the Pacific. I knew this treasure trove existed, but it was not given to me by my mother until a few years before her passing. In addition to providing a sense of the love my parents shared, these letters were most helpful to me in tracking living locations and time frames for certain events during the war years. The *second*, and perhaps most helpful and impressive to me, was the hands-on trip that my wife, Patty, and I took to Tucson, Bisbee, and Douglas, Arizona, and Agua Prieta, Mexico, the purpose of which was threefold: (1) to visit in Tucson some new extended family in my life from my father's side that I found through my research, and that have been so helpful to me in my efforts; (2) to visit firsthand some of the Douglas locations, neighborhoods, Catholic church, nuns' private residence, and Catholic school that played such influential roles in and made lifelong impressions upon my father's early years and later character development; and (3) to explore Agua Prieta with our guides Sr. Bernardo Morales, Mexican Consulate Director, located in Douglas, Arizona, and his friend and Agua Prieta historian, Sr. Juan Valente Rivera Aguirre, both of whom were very helpful and knowledgeable in taking my wife and me to specific locations from my father's story.

My personal research effort, plus living and growing up in our family and having first- and secondhand knowledge of some of my father's later-life recollections, helped me greatly in providing for the record a more complete written story, including essential, numerous photographic images with my explanatory, contextual captions of places, people, and events for reader understanding and appreciation. These images are placed at the beginning of each Book Part, at the end of some chapters, and/or three of the Book Part conclusions. Please note that some names have been changed and certain recollections filtered to preserve privacy and/or tone down more salacious memories. And, finally, the narrative is written in the first person so that the spirit of my father's writing and our collaboration remains intact.

To those present and future generations of our family and friends, and all other interested persons, enjoy and appreciate my father's personal history and experiences, especially the very significant early years, his final separation and growing away from those difficult times, becoming a young adult, then entering early manhood, eventually marrying and becoming a husband and father, and leaving his roots behind as he continued his assimilation into the social culture at large. My parents lovingly created a life together and a happy home for my siblings and me that lasted throughout most of our growing up into adulthood.

Thank you Father and Mother for your many gifts! And God bless you Dad, Mom, Richard Jr., and Sherry Lynn. I daily love and miss each of you!

Your loving son and brother, Anthony

My brother Richard Jr. in back, my sister Sherry Lynn sitting, and me in the middle. Family portrait photo was taken in 1987. My sister's illness was diagnosed the following day. Family photo album.

A Mother and Son's Wanderings in Arizona and Mexico
1927–1933

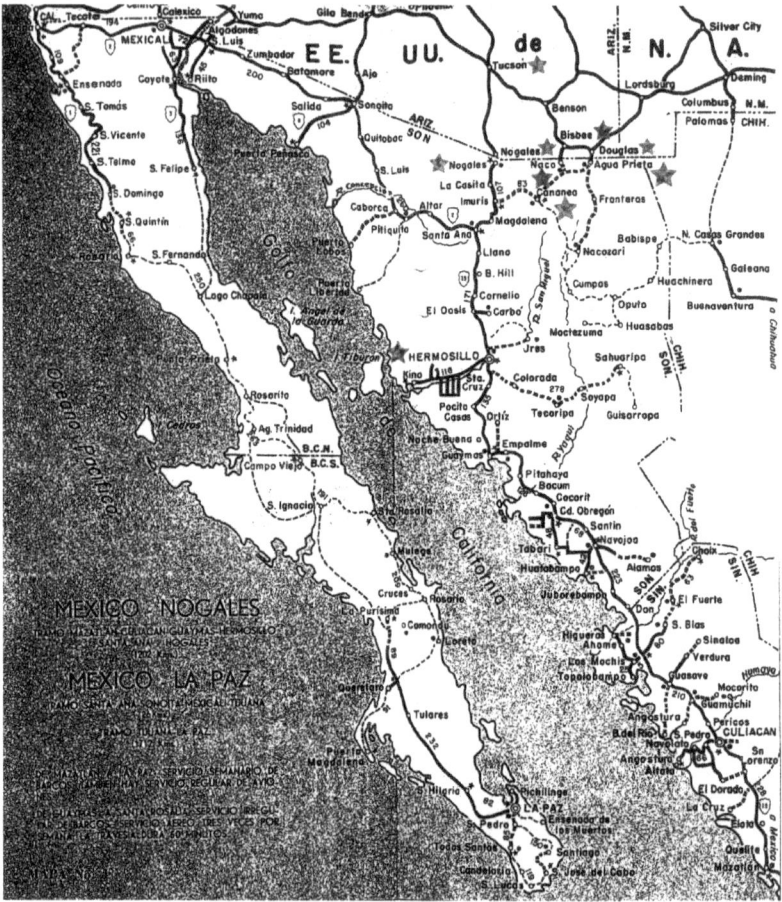

This mid-twentieth century map of Mexico, Sonora, and its border with southern Arizona, provides the geographical areas continuously traveled by my father and his mother, highlighted with shaded stars placed next to the city name. Notice that there are also smaller towns on the roads traveled that I would guess they stopped in from time to time, though my father does not mention others specifically. Map is provided courtesy of a Mexican corporation wishing to remain anonymous.

Son's Prologue

A GUIDE TO THIS MEMOIR'S VERGARA, HUMPHREYS, AND HERNANDEZ RELEVANT FAMILY RELATIONSHIPS

(Richard E. Hernández Sr.'s maternal grandparents)
Antonio Vergara / First wife Clotilde Islava
Children born in order:
- Magdalena
- Trini
- Gilda
- *Guadalupe* (my father's mother)

Antonio Vergara / Second wife Margarita Garcia
Children born in order:
- Emma
- Antonio Jr.
- Amalia
- Albert
- Robert

All above Vergara family members deceased.

(Richard's future wife and my mother Janet's family)
Nicholas John Humphreys / wife Violet May Nelson
Children born in order:
- Violet
- Edward
- Janet
- Beverly
- Jack
- Charles
- Calvin

All above Humphreys family members deceased.

(Parents of my father Richard E. Hernández)
Edmundo Hernández Sr. / wife Guadalupe Vergara
Child born:
- Ricardo Edmundo Hernández Jr.

On August 1, 1942, Richard E. Hernández marries Janet Anne Humphreys
Children born in order:
- Richard Jr.
- Sherry Lynn
- *Anthony*

All above Hernández family members are deceased except Anthony, now seventy-eight years old.

FATHER'S INTRODUCTION

THIS WAS NOT MY IDEA. But I reacted to the many requests my son Tony had made to me to please let my two sons know how we all got here to this time and place. For me to recall just how it was that I arrived to this place at this time was certainly not easy and very emotional for me; it was difficult to try and remember my passing life and to go back possibly seventy years and form a sense of history of all of my unhappy and traumatic times growing up.

My life is a statement, at least to me and my two sons and deceased daughter, that despite being raised under some very difficult circumstances as an only child with an alcoholic parent, and never having the privilege of knowing a home, a person can endure many hardships and still be a good and responsible citizen to the community in which you live. The scars will always be within and will occasionally show, but only to one's self, not to everybody else. My burdensome scars were my missed opportunities for a formal education during my early and developing years, and lack of a stable home to enable me to fully appreciate what life had to offer as I grew up.

So in my marriage, as a husband and father as my children grew up, I devoted myself, along with my wife, to the making of a steady and respectable family life so that our children would be responsible, contributing adults in their lives and in their families, as well as in their communities. I was not the perfect parent, far from it, nor husband in later life, but my children were blessed with an adoring and faithful, honest, superhuman being for a mother and a wife. And she made us whole.

PART ONE

1927-1933

The Toughest Years—Two Insignificant People Living Insignificant Lives

Guadalupe Vergara, my grandmother, age twenty-five, and my father Ricardo, age three. This is from an enhanced photo taken from a required border crossing card, dated September 14, 1925. Their Port of Arrival was Nogales, Arizona, coming from Nogales, Mexico. In 2015 I found this photo through Ancestry.com research; it was the first time I had ever seen a photo of my grandmother, let alone with my father. Needless to say I was overwhelmed with emotion having found what is now one of my personal treasures. This photo was made available to me through my efforts with the National Archives located in Seattle and using Ancestry.com source material to track down digitized microfilm and having it sent from Denver National Archives to Seattle. I was able to make copies, which I then took to a local camera shop with digital expertise to make image reproductions of what was a very poor picture to begin with; what you see above is a vast improvement. Photo courtesy of Ancestry.com.

---

1   The National Archives and Records Administration; Washington D.C.; Nonstatistical Manifests and Statistical Index Cards of Aliens Arriving at Douglas, Arizona, July 1908–December 1952; NAI: 2843448; Record Group Title: Records of the Immigration and Naturalization Service, 1787–2004.; Record Group Number: 85; Microfilm Roll Number: 4.

CHAPTER ONE

My early childhood years that I think I remember best are from 1927 to 1933. So many things are erratic, but since there was never a home base from which to start and end, mostly all that I remember are things that come to mind as they happened. My mother and I never had roots, only sometimes we were lucky to stay at this or that place for two to three days, maybe a week. My mother was so unsettled and alcoholism was her biggest problem. She was truly a woman of her world. She was in her early twenties and loved a good time; being a mother was a sometime thing. To put little happenings together is the hard part; there will be a memory here and a memory there.

These early years were the most sorrowful and impressive on my childhood because I was a street kid, probably on the loose, and most likely not seeing my mother for days at a time. I have no idea what happened to school years in my life for this span of time; most likely I didn't attend. When I really think of where I grew up, I would have to say everyplace, primarily the state of Sonora, Mexico, where our adventures took place in the towns and on the streets of Agua Prieta, Cananea, Hermosillo, Naco, and Nogales. Towns in Arizona included Tucson, Nogales, Douglas, and Bisbee. We would travel in passenger cars that were the buses that transported travelers to these little towns; they were the older touring sedans. People had their chickens, belongings, and other personal pots and pans collected as baggage. Of course we had the clothes on our backs and maybe a peso or two, but in those years a peso was real money. The exchange rate then was two pesos to the dollar. Also, in those days a woman was always catered to by the lonesome men; my mother and these men would just send me off someplace to buy candy. But you must realize that I was knowledgeable about getting by and I could take care of myself. Once you become adept at survival, one city is like another.

These were the busy years for my childhood. There were a lot of things that I did know about my extended family. I had an aunt in Nogales, Mexico, Aunt Magdalena Espinosa. She had six or seven kids, including boys and girls; her husband, Ramon was a mechanic for the bus company. Ramon was a short, stocky man, balding a little, and always wore a *cachucha*, Spanish for cap. This cap was not a sport's cap—those didn't exist—but rather was a cap made for dress or work, and most men wore these. The bus company where Ramon worked was a city transportation system comprised of regular buses. But, also in the Nogales, Mexico, system were hundreds of what people called *trambillas*. These were converted Model T pick-ups made into a sort of small bus. They had a cover over the back with benches on either side and steps for passengers to get on. They were colorfully painted to the owners' tastes, very attractive and happy looking as well as cheap to ride. Nogales, Mexico, is the only place these vehicles were seen by me; I don't believe they crossed the border into the United States.

Aunt Magdalena was a homemaker, and we called her Nena as an endearing family nickname. Her children ranged in years, with about half being the older ones about my age at that time, eight or nine years old. Aunt Nena would clean me all up every time I came by and would take care of me. I'd stay with them a few days and she'd always say to me, "Ricardo, you should be going to school, and if your mother would live here with us, I'd send you to school." She'd say, "*¿Madre de Dios, que vamos hacer con Lupita tu mama?*" Mother of God, what are we going to do with your mother?

This would be 1930 or 31. The Depression was just getting tough in the United States and things were as bad or worse in Nogales, Mexico. A family of eight was not easy for Ramon to support, but they would have been happy to keep me with them.

Aunt Nena's older daughter, Eva—we called her Evita—might have been just a little older than me. She was beginning to experience sexual stirrings within, and I seemed to be a good source of excitement to her. She would want me to play house with her, which I obligingly did. The big, old house in which the family lived was two or three stories high and was surrounded by trees just as tall that extended over the roof, making some rather nice, dark hiding places. She and I would climb the trees and hide among the branches and would play "you show me yours and I'll show you mine." We were two young and curious kids discovering the mysteries of human anatomy. We would giggle, touch, and laugh and feel good and naughty all at the same time. Evita seemed more ready for such discovery than I was, though nothing ever went beyond our childish curiosity. Afterward we would return to inside the house and giggle and say we would do it again. The times when I could stay with the Espinosa family were fun, and I have good and warm memories of those moments. It was very sad when I had to leave to experience another of life's adventures that my mother ceaselessly provided me.

I also had an aunt in Nogales, Arizona, Aunt Trini and Uncle Enrique Ainza. Aunt Trini would go to Nogales, Mexico, and visit with Aunt Nena so, from time to time, eventually I'd end up at Aunt Trini's. They had four kids, including Manuel, Arsenio, and Armeda; the fourth's name I do not remember. Aunt Trini's family lived in a house on a hillside located in a very nice neighborhood. The house was a white Cape Cod with three bedrooms and a basement with a garage. They had all the things that I equated with being rich: clean neighborhood, sidewalks, and paved streets. To me, they were very prosperous looking. Uncle Enrique was a very handsome and debonair gentleman, while Aunt Trini just looked and showed class. They were most kind to me and liked to help me and would have provided the same to my mother if she would have just given them a chance. Enrique was a salesman; I always thought he was a good salesman because he looked so successful at whatever he sold, so he must have been good. It is only recently that I found out that he used to sell animal fat (processed lard), which he smuggled into Mexico from the United States. I guess at that time lard was hard to get in Mexico, so he found a market for it and filled a need. Whatever he did, it seemed to me this family had everything. Enrique drove a beautiful black sedan, which always sparkled neat and clean.

During my infrequent stays at Aunt Trini's, her children, being close to my age, though I was maybe a little older than they, were so good to me as they really must have realized that I was very poor. I don't think that they would have known about my mother, but regardless, they just made me feel at home and couldn't do enough for me. I remember them asking Aunt Trini why I didn't go to school and she would say that I went to school in Mexico where I lived. When I visited with my aunts, they always gave me either a very short haircut or a pig shave because I was so infested with both head and body lice since some of the places and/or families with whom I stayed were probably as infested with lice as I was. My aunts would strip me down of all my dirty clothes and either burn them or boil them to kill the lice. You have to understand that since I was sleeping wherever I could, I hardly ever bathed and my clothes were always dirty. I can't imagine when or how I would take a bath or get clean clothes. I suppose I wore whatever clothes I had on for long stretches of time. When I would leave my aunts, I always had clean, nice hand-me-down clothes and shoes to wear, both of which never seemed to last long once I left.

What a fortunate young boy I was to have such supportive relatives as they suffered through my mother's alcoholism. The relatives from my mom's side of the family, her sisters and my grandparents, were a proud bunch and very respectable people. When Trini would go visit Nena, they would talk about Mom and demonstrate compassion for the way she was and lived. For me it is so hard to visualize that these two good women were sisters to my mother, a person who was so dysfunctional. Trini and Nena would fuss over me and want to keep me with them, but it just never happened. When my mom did come to pick me up, they would express their concern over my welfare and actually threaten to hide me from her. Of course, that's all Mom had to hear and off we'd go. I know that Trini and Nena were both brokenhearted, but there was nothing that they were able to do to change my mother's behavior.

Son, you must not think ill of my relatives; they always tried to take care of me and help me, to feed and clothe me. But my mother did not want them meddling in her life, so she stayed as far away from them as she could. There were many times when we would be in Nogales, Arizona, and I would make my way to family and hang on as long as I could, but my mom always came and got me and off we would go once again into our world of homelessness and survival.

*My father Ricardo at two years of age.
Photo from my father's treasured possessions.*

My father's aunts Magdalena, age 29, and Trini, age 40. Both photos taken from border crossings dated 1923 and 1936, respectively left to right. Magdalena was coming from Nogales, Mexico, to Nogales, Arizona. Trini was traveling from Mexicali, Mexico to Calexico, California. Courtesy of Ancestry.com.

---

2   The National Archives and Records Administration; Washington D. C.; *Index and Manifests of Alien Arrivals at Nogales, Arizona, July 5, 1905–1952*; NAI: *2843448*; Record Group Title: *Records of the Immigration and Naturalization Service, 1787-2004.*: Record Group Number: *85*; Microfilm Roll Number: *74*.
3   Ibid. Record Group Number: *85*; Microfilm Roll Number: *53*.

CHAPTER TWO

I guess that our most frequented area of activity would have to have been Agua Prieta and Nogales, both in the state of Sonora, Mexico, where a large part of our wanderings occurred. There were so many places in the surrounding towns that one could get to merely by first making friends with the car drivers, and my mother had a knack for that. My mother was a very pretty woman and of course was young and friendly. I suppose that having a little kid with her gave her a better opportunity to have men take pity on us both and to feel sorry for her. You must know that those years were hard times in Mexico.

When I was not with my mom, which was most of the time, I would ask for pennies from the Americans going to shop in Agua Prieta. A penny could buy a gingerbread cookie. We called them *cochitos* because they were made in the form of little pigs; they were good. When somebody gave me a nickel, that was better yet; I could buy a burrito, a taco, or a Mexican drink called *orchata* made from milk, crushed ice, rice, and cinnamon. My biggest concern was that when it started to get dark, it was time to start looking for a friend, another little guy who probably had a place that he called home, and to whom I could attach myself. And of course, once his mother would find out I had no place to go home to, I was able to get a meal and most likely a bed for the night. Also, with my luck, I could stay more than one night, maybe three nights, then somehow my mother would find me.

As I remember, these small towns did not require you to go a long way to get around. There were the downtown area stores, markets, all sorts of vendors, and if you were going to hustle somebody out of a penny or something to eat, this was the place to do it.

Of course the cantinas, taverns, and drinking parlors were also in this area; a sure place to find my mom. Her favorite spot in Agua Prieta was a cantina called Los Pajaritos, the little birds, because the white stucco exterior building had hundreds of little birds painted on it. I recall lots of drinking, noise, music, and singing.

I remember so vividly an American whose name was Jim Douglas, a plumber, and he had a crippled leg and always wore bib overalls and a hat. He also had a green car, a coupe it was, probably a 1927 or 1929 Buick or Dodge, which had black fenders, big wheels and tires and a rumble seat. Every time I saw this car it was always nice and clean. My mother met this good man in Agua Prieta and developed a relationship with him. To me Jim Douglas was somewhat special in a way. He was a kind, strong, and compassionate man. At the time I didn't know what all those words meant, but he showed strength and kindness when other men were out for what they could get from my mother. To these other men, I was just a kid in the way of their personal needs. Jim, on the other hand, stood out from these other types of men. In him I saw a sincerity that I had not noticed in other men in my mother's life.

Jim was an Anglo who spoke a little Spanish, probably as a result of living in border towns and being around the language. He was a little older than my mother, maybe thirty-five to forty years old.

Two Insignificant People Living Insignificant Lives

I do not know how he came to be with my mother and me. But, I do believe that he thought enough of her to rent a place for us in which to stay in Agua Prieta, and he would come to visit often. How long we stayed in this rented place I cannot tell you. When Jim visited, he would bring something for my mom and usually a nickel for me, give me a pat on the head, and ask me if I was taking care of Mom. Sometimes he would bring us things to eat from his home in Douglas. Other times he would ask me if I was going to go to the store to spend the money he gave me, so I would say "OK," but first I would ask him if I could get into his car. He'd say "*Si*, yes, you can but don't let other kids get in the car with you, and be sure to lock the doors." I loved that car and relished my time playing in it while Jim visited my mother. When Jim would leave, my mother would have money, which he would have given her, and she would use this to buy alcohol. I don't seem to recall both of them drinking during his visits, only that he left money that she would later use to support her addiction. In my eyes, Jim was a very respectable man, a good role model, and impressed me anyway.

Jim was the only person I knew at that time in my life who was so rich. He must have been, as a lot of men still rode horses and wagons, a sight not uncommon in Mexico during those times; it was a country light years behind the United States. I believe that Jim Douglas lived in a brick apartment complex, sort of U shaped, one story with several units, having a grass courtyard in the middle with trees, very clean, orderly, and located in a nice neighborhood. I say nice because in contrast to Agua Prieta, this part of Douglas, Arizona, had sidewalks, paved streets, curbs, and planted trees along the street.

When my mother and I sneaked across the border to visit my mom's uncle Trinidad Islava, sometimes we would go to Jim's place just to visit. In his home there was such order in everything and what a display of personal wealth. I thought that he was very rich; in Spanish we would say *"muy rico."* It is unfortunate that my mother didn't know how to latch on to a man of his caliber on a permanent basis. In all the years Mom and I lived together, I can't recall another man in her life who was cut from the same cloth.

Two Insignificant People Living Insignificant Lives

Border crossing from Douglas, Arizona, USA, in the back ground; Agua Prieta, Mexico, in the foreground, linked through the one highway going north and south. Border facilities for the United States are located in the one- and two-story facilities on the right in the distance. The Mexican facility located just off-center to the left of the photo, and the trees planted at lower foreground, were adjacent to additional Mexican border crossing support functions. My dad used to panhandle next to the park area corner at the right of the trees next to the highway, as people traveled by on their way to Agua Prieta to shop, visit, or return home. See Chapter 7, for a postcard photo looking toward the Mexican administrative facilities; the above image was taken from that building's roof. Note roof protrusions lower left. Early twentieth century photograph courtesy of www.apsoncezar.com.

Time period vista view of Agua Prieta courtesy www.apsoncezar.com.

Los Pajaritos Restaurant located at Esquina Calle 4 and 4th Avenue, Agua Prieta. Photo taken by my wife during our October 2015 trip to Arizona and Mexico. Photo taken from the NE corner of the intersection of Calle 4 and 4th Ave. looking to the SW corner of 4th Ave. (white van on left) and Calle 4 (white SUV on right).

I believe this photo provides a period picture of Los Pajaritos, shown a tad off-center to the left, being the white, one-story building with cars parked out front on the dirt street. The address of the photo is the same as provided above. Photo is taken on 4th Avenue just south of the same building shown in the above photo. Courtesy of www.apsoncezar.com.

CHAPTER THREE

So many memories just come to mind that don't seem to fit in any particular place, but these are things that I experienced during the tough years of my young life as we traveled from small town to small town for whatever reason my mother had. Most of her wanderings, I believe, stemmed from the idea that that time of our lives was going to be free of family interference. She did not wish for our relatives to be really aware of her failures in life. Many unhappy and bad experiences became part of our lives due to our unsettled family life. People that could take advantage, especially men, did just that. In my young experience I learned there are always people, mostly men, that prey on weaker persons, especially women, and are the opportunists.

In the 1920s, the years that I remember more vividly because of the tough times in Sonora, Mexico, there were salesmen who sold their wares such as yards of cloth, pots and pans, tools, hardware, dresses, and soaps. These wares were carted on wagons, hitched to either small bands of burros, mules, or horses, traveling a route from small villages to other small villages that were isolated from railroads, bus lines, and normal foot traffic.

One particular time my mother decided that we would go to

Cananea, Sonora. Because we had no money, she thought we could hitchhike. I was probably six or seven and what she said went. By hitchhiking she meant that whatever became available we would accept that chance to keep from walking, whether cars, wagons, a ride on a donkey, or whatever. This particular time a man going to a small village to sell his wares came upon us, and my mom saw an opportunity to hitch a ride. So we each got on a donkey packing the salesman's wares. After several miles we came to this small place, a distillery for mescal and tequila. Of course they needed the cactuses to distill in order to make the stuff. There were several men working at the distillery, with fires burning under giant cauldrons, and steam was coming from all of them. It was basically a rough and tough bunch of degenerates and depraved men, all, of course, drunk most of the time. There may have been a family or two, maybe a few more, but they were apart from the distillery. I was afraid of what I perceived was going to happen. Remember, living like we did, I'd seen almost everything that life could offer regarding drunkenness and sex.

In this camp they had food for the men that lived and worked there. So there was food and drink, tequila and mescal for the adults, soda for me. My mom was in seventh heaven. All you could drink and fun too; one woman, ten degenerates, and one small, scared little guy, me. When the party picked up and everybody was drunk, the other thing to do was to rape that beautiful, young lady. I've never forgotten the fight I put up trying to save my mom. It only took one or two drunk guys to hold me while the others held my mother's arms and legs and they all raped her. My mom fought, but heck, she was drunk and most likely did not know what happened. I know because I watched it all, crying and screaming to leave her alone, but those drunken sons of bitches wouldn't. I know that they are all dead by now and I hope that their souls rot in hell! This is one of several emotional chapters in my life and one that I hated most of all to write about. It's hard for me to remember how we left there, I suppose by the same means that brought us there. It had been just another episode in a struggling life of two unimportant human beings; this was our life and it had to be lived the only way that my mother knew how.

There are lots of bits and pieces of my life that come to mind as I write specific memories. Some are brief recollections that are a part of my experience, a few of which are very emotional for me and I must stop to gather myself. These are the real parts of my life that only I knew and experienced. Others are more complete in my memory and I am able to more thoroughly recount the experience. I am talking about our travels, which sometimes were never-ending. Travels to destinations unknown, the towns we were going to were always just ahead of us, and sometimes when we got to our destination, we were just passing through. My mother and I just never seemed to settle anywhere; that need was not in my mom's thinking.

My mother was an alcoholic and a woman of the streets, but it was impossible for her to be drunk twenty-four hours a day. It was during those sober times that I saw a mother who loved her child and was really deeply concerned about my welfare, if only for a little while. She would ask me if I was hungry or cold, thirsty or tired, and she would always say we'll be getting to this or that town pretty soon and then we will be just fine. My mom always had ways of providing; sometimes she would play on peoples' sympathy and she could get a small portion of something to eat for her little man. These moments of being a mother would disappear when she found something to drink, at which time I would go into my survival mode because I knew I might not see her for some time. My mom just made a bad choice as to how to live her life when she was very young, perhaps twenty to twenty-two years of age. By the time I started to be able to see how we lived, I was five years old or about; my mom was then about twenty-six years of age.

My mother had her problems that were far beyond simple solving. She must have suffered anxiety resulting from not knowing what to do and how best to do it. This must have been coupled with a sense of hopelessness and being overwhelmed with the responsibilities of trying to care for her son, while all the time thinking where was her next drink coming from, because that was her escape route.

She could be very abusive when she was drunk and would beat the hell out of me with the heel of her shoe. Maybe that is why I have so many bumps on my skull. My guess would be that during those times she felt she had to take her anger out on someone; I was always there. Alcoholics that are either on the wagon or about to be drunk can be very unreasonable. Also, can you imagine how a woman with a child must feel when she has to face reality and realize that life could be different someway? That it could be better than how we lived, and there doesn't seem to be anybody who really cares? That life is beyond reach and impossible to improve? Through drinking you escape all those problems, and the longer you can stay drunk, the less you have to worry about life and how you might change.

So what you do when you can't change is you change the scenery and move on. When my mom said we were going, we would leave right then. You have to understand that these interactions and conversations did not take place in a home setting, rather she would run into me or I would run into her on the street and we were on our way again, this time to Hermosillo from Nogales, Mexico.

Hermosillo is about ninety kilometers, a little more than 115 miles, from Nogales, Mexico. When transportation is a problem, it might as well be at the end of the earth. Hermosillo, how many rides and days will it take to get there? We are talking now about 1930, a seven- or eight-year-old boy, whose poor feet must walk mostly without shoes. I am sure it was no picnic for my mother either. One thing we did not have was much luggage to carry, maybe a paper sack, although I don't know what would have been in it; in those days we didn't have plastic bags. I don't know how many miles we walked. We would hitch a ride in a horse-pulled wagon, or an old car or truck here and there, and walk on hot sand, dirt, or blacktop. I am sure I complained; being hungry was, of course, part of the trip. If it wasn't one thing to complain about, it was another. Most of the time we did not have any water, and as far as having the foresight to take along something to eat, well somehow that was not a priority. Our trips were never planned, without any consideration of being sensible.

And now she and I looked around and for a hundred miles you could see the desert heat waves above the blacktop, sagebrush everywhere, hot sand to walk on, and the glaring sun. It was very lonely on this Mexican road, hardly any traffic. Far off in the distance I saw an outline of a hill and wondered, "What is over that hill, and besides, would there be something to eat there?" My little mind was bored with hunger, thirst, and exhaustion, and when I complained, *"Estoy hambriento,"* I am hungry, my mom would say, *"Esperate hijo."* Wait my son. I was lagging behind and all of a sudden she said, *"Mira hijo, lo que me aye."* Look son what I found.

I asked her, "*Que te ayaste mamma?*" What did you find, mamma? She replied, "*Un cacahuate, hijo,*" I found a peanut. Then she said, "*Y tiene tres nueces, dos para ti y una para mi.*" And it has three nuts, two for you and one for me. (Wow, this is most emotional for me and there are some tears to flow with this recollection.) She and I ate the peanut and savored the taste. It was sweet and flavorful and now I said to her, "*Mamma, las nueces son muy sabrosas.*" Mom, the nuts are very tasty. We continued walking, hoping that a ride would come; a car came by and there it went, getting smaller as it got farther away. Those people that just passed by were not heartless, just preoccupied with their own concerns and problems. A woman and a little boy just walking in the desert was not a prime concern because that was not unusual; two people grasping at hope and a way to survive. Telling these things and writing about these small parts of my life is painful, but if a person does not have emotions that touch one's very soul, one might as well be dead. Finally, I don't remember specifically how we got to Hermosillo.

My mother and I had been to Hermosillo before when I was younger, maybe one or two years earlier. Somehow the area we headed to was the market, a most beautiful and big place with lots of marble pillars and white tile floors, and many people. This I am sure of: to me it was the most impressive setting, with people selling all their wares, vegetables, and meats; chickens and rabbits hanging; banners and flags flying, with signs and a festival atmosphere; everybody wearing colorful clothing. I could get lots of things to eat there also. As for my mom, her system needed something to drink; she would start looking for a watering hole and let the good times roll. And for me, survival began again. Hermosillo was an easy place in which to do that because food was plentiful there and somebody always took pity and gave the poor kids something to eat.

I was not the only youngster on the street at that time. There were lots of kids, all most likely trying to survive a similar situation as mine. For me, these hard times sometimes could be fun and happiness was just having a full tummy and playing with others my age. There was lots of joy because there were mariachis singing and playing beautiful music. Mexican music can be very emotional and to this day my eyes tear when I hear some of the old songs and music that I would hear in the cantinas and taverns where and when I would be looking for my mom. I would be concerned for her if I hadn't seen her for several days. Little kids need loving and some tenderness even when they are capable of enduring loneliness and hunger. There was still love for that person who was my mother.

Hermosillo. Somehow I heard, and I can't remember where or when, that my mom had died in Hermosillo; she had to have been at least seventy-five or eighty years old. She was a woman who had abused herself so terribly—all the drinking, all the meals she never ate, sicknesses she must have had, and, I am sure, ever so lonely. As I think of how she must have existed in her later years, it now brings tears to my eyes because I wasn't there to do anything. I could have done something had I known, but I never made an effort. I suppose I wouldn't have known where to start. May God have mercy on her soul.

Hermosillo, Calle Serdán, 1928. Most likely my father and his mother walked this major city street during their several visits, at times together and others perhaps not. Courtesy of mexicoenfotos/yayozarate.

Time period photo of the Hermosillo Municipal Public Market and a location my father was confident he could get something to eat while panhandling to passersby. This photo hangs in a restaurant within the Mercado Municipal and thanks to Sr. Bernardo Morales, permission to use was provided courtesy of the restaurant management.

CHAPTER FOUR

I stop during my writings and ponder the many minute things that happened, and how all of these things put together make up a life. I wonder how I survived the hunger, the loneliness, or the need for ordinary things. I first see myself as a little guy following a mother who had no idea what she wanted with her life, but she always wanted me with her when she had her mental faculties and was sober. Son, at this moment I recollect a saying your grandfather had. He would say I don't know where I am going but I am on my way. And so we were on our way from Hermosillo to wherever.

Wherever that was, was not far. It could be fifteen, seventy-five, or one hundred miles, but to me what did I know? The towns might as well have been a thousand miles away for it was just another milestone in my experiences. This one time my mother and I were on another trip through life; how we ended up at this place I can't tell you, probably walking down a road, waiting for a ride. My mom asked somebody where we were or was a town close by. We were invited to this person's home and his family was there. They were all Chinese, lived in an older home, and included his wife and four kids about my age. The home consisted of a small plot of land, some outbuildings, and wheat, which they raised in their fields. That was a new experience for me. My mother and I stayed at this place maybe one or two weeks. We ate very well, and I remember when we sat down at the table, there were what seemed to me to be hundreds of dishes, all filled with vegetables, greens, and meats such as chicken, beef, and others. The food was tasty, good, and flavorful and my mother was sober, no drinking here and no place to go to get booze. Of course, it goes without saying but these Chinese folks spoke Spanish, so communication was not a concern. It was an experience for me that has never diminished from my mind, this small family struggling, as were the times, to make a living out of hard work and successfully doing so.

This Chinese family harvested wheat with hand scythes; they all did this as a family and one day invited me to participate. I was so proud to be harvesting wheat with a hand scythe, bunching it up and putting it into a pile. There were wheat fields as far as I could see, yellow wheat almost as tall as me. I watched how his kids did it and this Chinese man showed me what to do. Heck, I was probably seven years old at the time and anxious to learn. I felt in my mind that I owed this man something, so I worked extra hard. I guess my mom must have helped the lady with the housework. When we labored in the fields, this lady and my mom brought meals for us to eat—three a day, what a treat! My mom was sober and there were clean clothes for me! It just didn't get any better!

Squirrels. Every time I see a squirrel I think of our stay with this family. One day the Chinese man made me a slingshot. I did not know anything about slingshots, but the kids showed me how to shoot it. And now, here we all went to the woods, the man, his kids, and me. He had a twenty-two caliber rifle and we kids all had slingshots; we were going someplace to do something in the woods. That something turned out to be hunting squirrels for meat. The meat in the meals that we had been eating was chicken, rabbit, and squirrel; good too, the way his wife fixed them. Their system of hunting was unique. The boys would line up and scramble through the brush and the ground squirrels would run up the trees while we shot at them with our slingshots. Once the squirrel was up the tree, the man would shoot it with his rifle. We came home with squirrels to eat, which was one of the staples of this family's diet. To this day Chinese food is my most favorite food, with the exception of the squirrel.

It was a pleasant stay here with those Chinese folks. I had a good time playing with the kids and without access to alcohol my mom was a real mom. It could have been two to three weeks we stayed with this family, and then it was time to hit the road to life in another world. When we left this home, I was sad because their lifestyle was so different from mine and I liked how they lived. Of course, we could not stay there indefinitely, so we left to return to more familiar territory. Later in life I learned that in the early nineteenth century Chinese immigrants traveled to both Hermosillo and Cananea, Mexico, either from China or through the United States, to work in the copper mines that had been established there. I suppose that the family with whom we stayed may have had some connection to that experience. Seems possible.

Upon leaving the Chinese family, we found ourselves in a farming community. I believe wheat might have been the money crop. Shipping this wheat to market was a big job and was done using huge horse-drawn wagons that were taken toward the border with the United States. My guess is that there were fifteen to twenty horses pulling each wagon. Cananea, about thirty miles southwest of the border town of Naco, Mexico, was a destination traveled to by these wagons. Hitchhiking as we always did, a small convoy of wheat wagons caught up with us. There might have been five or six of them. My mom and I were offered a ride and to me that seemed exciting. Just to climb upon the wagon was a hell of a job for a little guy like me. My mother and I sat way up high on top and the driver sat in the front. These wagons were probably ten feet high and quite wide, with huge wheels. The driver wore a big brim straw hat to keep the sun out of his face. He had a big whip and to get the wagon started he'd pop the whip over the horses' heads. The giant wheels would creak and the driver would holler *haaaaay*! Boy, was that exciting! And with the comfort of the soft wheat to lie on and the creaking of the wagon wheels, I am sure with a little nap I could forget the big world outside. There was water to drink from canvas bags; that type of container always kept the water cool. The drivers gave us something to eat, beef jerky (*carne seca*) and bread. At the next little town our ride ended because the drivers and the horses had to rest and wait the night there. We might have ridden fifteen to twenty miles, maybe less. I do know it was a slow pace because the wagons were loaded heavy, though the horses were used to this type of work. They were strong, big, and well cared for.

Cananea was our destination close to more familiar territory. As I remember, it was a small, crowded town with lots of horses and wagons, and a few automobiles, mostly trucks and Model Ts and As. There were many donkeys and mules doing their work, with lots of people on the streets, including numerous kids probably not much better off than me. Also, there were many cantinas. My mom had been on the wagon for a long time, so this town was going to be heaven to her. At the time I did not know what made that town move, but I can tell you lots of drinking was done there.

Maybe there were distilleries making tequila mescal, the one with the worm. Right downtown was a beehive of activity. I didn't wander too far from that part of town because though I'd been to Cananea before, I didn't know the place. I just knew where a kid could get something to eat and that my mom was always where the action was.

I remember the city jail building and right behind it was a bridge coming down from a street up above. In the same place where the jail was located was a small hospital or first aid station to take care of the drunks in town. I cannot remember whether my mom had been in jail many times or not; she may have been when I was not with her, I just do not recall. This particular time in Cananea I do remember she was put in jail and I happened to be with her. Maybe she was put in jail because she was drunk or maybe because I was with her and the police wanted me off of the streets. I was allowed to see her after she was sober. I could visit her in jail while I stayed in a room next to the emergency entrance to the first aid station.

When I came to visit, she looked bad, unkempt, with unruly hair and a hangover. I am sure she did not know where I had spent the night or the day. She looked at me and stroked my head and said, *"Mi hijito a donde estavas?"* My son, where were you? *"Comiste este dia?"* Have you eaten today? I said, *"Si mamma, yo estaba ayi cerca de usted."* Yes, mother, I was real close to you over there in another room. Here was my mom with a hangover and not feeling well but yet concerned about my well-being. These are the times that tears come easy for me because at times she had the capability to be a mother and worry about me. God bless her soul.

I had to tell my mom about the experience I'd had while sleeping in the room adjoining the emergency entrance to the first aid station. I was in this small room and it had a window looking right into the carport where the ambulance pulled in to unload the injured. While I was in that room, I heard the ambulance pull into the carport and heard men's voices and rapid talking. I stepped out of bed and pulled aside the curtains and peered over the windowsill. The window was a little high for me, but what I saw scared the hell out of me because on the stretcher was a man, bare chested, arms at his side, and a knife sticking out of his chest. Of course, he must have been dead. I pulled the curtains closed and shut my eyes. I couldn't sleep the rest of the night.

I suppose my mom and I were there two days, no longer. I got fed by the police and they knew my mom was in jail, so they looked out for me. After they let Mom out, I also had to go, and into the streets again the two of us went. We left Cananea shortly thereafter, I guess, because they probably warned her that next time it would be a longer stay. Talk about ways and means. My mother had the ways to provide us with the means to be able to do something she wanted to do.

Two Insignificant People Living Insignificant Lives

1906 photo of Cananea; note the public park with gazebo in the foreground. I am quite certain that my father and grandmother would spend time in these parks that existed in all the towns and cities through which they traveled; they could rest and gather themselves. Or my father, most likely on his own, could maybe find other children to play with or someone to take pity on him and provide him a place to sleep or something to eat. Public domain photograph.

La Carcel De Cananea. Today this jail facility has been converted to the local historical museum. It would appear that the first aid station and/ or clinic my father mentions is located on the other side away from public view on the back side of the building. Note the street elevation on the right behind the jail; the access bridge must have come down from there. Courtesy of mexicoenfotos.com/centli.

CHAPTER FIVE

Agua Prieta was our most logical place to go after this stay in Cananea and long trip to Hermosillo, as Agua Prieta was the next larger town northeast. I seem to remember returning there more vividly after the Hermosillo trip mentioned above. I believe that is because I was older then. Even though my mom and I had been to Hermosillo many times before, this last trip leaves the strongest images, some scary, some happy.

Agua Prieta, Mexico, so familiar a town to me, opposite the border city of Douglas, Arizona. I think of all the places that I remember, and compared to other places my mother and I spent time in, I recall this particular one more. I believe it was because I was comfortable being there as I knew the area better and I felt at home even though we didn't live there. I had learned exactly where to panhandle and knew more kids there. Some of these youngsters were probably as bad off as I was. A few of them were acquaintances I had stayed with several times and their mothers had fed me on many occasions. Home is where the heart is, as the saying goes, but if you don't have a home, then it must be the most familiar place. For me, this place was Agua Prieta.

Two Insignificant People Living Insignificant Lives

Around 1984, my second wife, Joan, and I, and my uncle Bobby Vergara and his wife, Maria, visited some of my memories by traveling to Douglas, Arizona, Agua Prieta, Sonora, Mexico, and Bisbee, Arizona. The Agua Prieta Immigration Building close to the border was still there surrounded by a wrought iron fence. The barbwire fence that separates the United States from Mexico might be a little newer, but it was still there. As we drove around Douglas and Agua Prieta, I spotted many places very familiar to me. The city park in Agua Prieta has a gazebo where the old-time bands used to play on Saturdays and Sunday evenings. The young men and ladies would stroll around the walkway in the park, holding hands and, of course, followed by an older chaperone watching their every move. We little children would run, playing and chasing each other around the gazebo while the colorfully dressed band played their lovely music. There would be vendors all around the park, selling tacos, tostados, tamales, Mexican cactus candy, sodas, and cotton candy; everyone there was having a most wonderful time. As poor as most of these people were, they had class. The young men respected the young ladies, which made the chaperone's job that much easier. As we left that area, I remembered that in the back of my young mind raced the ever-present question, "Where am I going to sleep tonight?" But because some of my friends' folks knew I had no home, I frequently got to go with them. That's what I mean when I say a familiar place can almost be home.

During our tour we drove by what I thought might be the Cantina Los Pajaritos where I could always find my mother most of the time. The poor soul enjoyed this place the most. We then drove through some neighborhoods close to downtown. I noticed such poverty and degradation of peoples' lives. Somehow I saw a lot of what I could have become. I saw men—I would say about my current age at the time of sixty-two—drunk, lying on the sidewalks or leaning against a wall, probably wondering what happened to their lives. But for the grace of God, that could have been me. Fortunately, back when I was that young boy, I was snatched from that future possibility by a short, little man in bib overalls, a blue jacket, and a brim hat, with a mustache and a shopping bag in each hand. His name was Miguel Mendoza and he and his wife, Maria, were from Douglas, Arizona; I will speak of my life with the Mendozas further on in my story.

Of all the border towns, Agua Prieta was my mom's favorite place to jump the fence and enter the United States. I don't really know why but many, many times we did just that, entered this country at night. We would cross the fence way out of town and walk to Douglas, Arizona. It was a long walk to get into town from the desert, through sagebrush and cactus plants. At that time the fence was probably ten feet high, with barbed wire strands of sharpened, twisted wire approximately eight inches apart to keep people out. Of course, I don't believe that back then as many people crossed the line as they do now; times and numbers of people were different.

This particular time after we crossed the border, the outskirts of Douglas were maybe a couple of miles away. Sand dunes, sagebrush, and cactuses, the small sticky ones with thorns were a problem, especially with no shoes and walking in the dark. We're talking middle of the night here, so my mother and I could spot the immigration officers if they should come with their car lights on. She and I never got caught. Getting across the border was weird in the dark. My mom would step on a strand of wire, hold another with her bare hands, and pull it up, and I would crawl through; then I would do the same for her. And now in my young mind we were illegal immigrants going to somewhere in Douglas, Arizona.

On our way to that somewhere as we were walking into a neighborhood in Douglas in the middle of the night, or maybe early dawn, I spotted a small tricycle just sitting on the sidewalk. I said to my mom, *"Mira mama, una tricicleta, quiero jugar con ella."* Look mama, there's a tricycle, I want to play with it. She said, *"No puedes porque es muy tarde y no es tuya."* You can't because it's too late and it isn't yours. As it turned out, I did take the tricycle a short way and did ride it a little bit and left it about a block away. Picture this: my mom is pulling me by the hand and I am pulling the tricycle by the handle, all three in a row. That incident is memorable to me because I never had a toy like that before. She and I continued on our way to somewhere.

There were some relations in Douglas, my mother's uncle Trinidad Islava, who owned and/or was employed in the G Avenue Grocery Store in Douglas. He was her uncle on my grandmother's side, my grandfather's first marriage. I understand my mom did not visit with him too much because he used to scold her about her lifestyle and about taking me all over; consequently, she gave that relative a wide berth. I most remember him because he was nice to me. He would give me candy and cookies from the store. But most of all, he teased me. When I sat down to eat cookies and milk, he would get behind me and, while I was enjoying my treat, he would tap me on my shoulder and call me. "Ricardo," he would say, and I'd turn around and he would scare the hell out of me when he'd say, "Boo!" He would have turned his eyelids inside out and his eyes would be red and scary. I do not remember him much more than that. I do know that his son Ricardo was my godfather when

I was baptized in the Church of The Immaculate Conception in Douglas.

The trips to Douglas normally did not last long. Our relatives were not that many and people that we knew, or rather that my mom knew, were few in this town. Somehow we got around, I can't remember how or who else we might have visited. Besides my mom certainly did not want the Islavas intruding into her private life, so short stays were typical. Of course, her uncle Trinidad Islava meant well and most likely gave my mom a little money when we came to visit. How she spent the money most likely was not how he wished. When we did come to Douglas, our lives were not the same as in Mexico, as we had a chance to enjoy life in a different way because of the relatives. Mother had to straighten up and behave and show them that she had a good side. I loved that because I didn't have to be a vagrant kid. These stays did not last long, but they were memorable and left their impression on me.

In Agua Prieta, our place of domicile, wherever that might have been, there was an army barracks, maybe what we might call an armory, a place for soldiers to stay. It was referred to as El Cuartel. Some soldiers were billeted there, most of whom had their women staying with them or could have, as the army allowed it. My mom met an army man there or most likely in a cantina, and they decided maybe she and I could stay and become a part of this action. Of course, I was a part of that reality. There were some kids that lived there because, as I mentioned, the soldiers could have their women with them. Some soldiers, however, did not have female companionship, so they would hustle random women who were willing to make themselves available to visit and perhaps stay for a few days. The soldiers would provide food, maybe some booze, and a place to sleep. For these privileges the women provided the enjoyment of their companionship to the many soldiers. From what I could tell of the situation, there were more than a few men to each woman. As for me, I enjoyed playing with the kids and getting fed too, as well as seeing the army equipment such as guns, trucks, and horses.

The real purpose of all the kindness displayed to us by the soldiers was the rewards they helped themselves to at night after some tequila and mescal. After the partying came the pleasures of life. My mom and I had a room where we slept on the floor on army blankets; most likely the ones the soldiers used for placing under the saddles. After dark, late in the night as my mom and I slept under the same blanket, the soldiers would arrive. Of course, I was supposed to be sound asleep and nothing would wake me up. Soldiers would come and visit my mother and have their pleasures with her, one after another, all the while my mind would be thinking, "I am supposed to be asleep and I mustn't act as if I am awake." But because of all the life that I had seen before this time, I knew about sex and what was happening here. I knew as much as anybody about life for my age, and I guess I reasoned in my mind that this was the way most people lived. However, as much as I had seen of life, this was as close as I had ever been to the sexual act. Many times I had been in the same house, but not in the same room, let alone in the same bed covered with the same blankets. I can remember covering my ears so I wouldn't hear everything; I suppose I eventually fell asleep.

As I reflect on this memory, I am keenly aware that as a youngster I never had a male role model to try and imitate. In some strange way, perhaps that helped me to form a value system that was the opposite from what I had seen throughout my life: life in the raw, people using other people, men using women in whichever way benefited them and their men friends. In my world I saw in men's minds and actions that they were mostly users, takers, and opportunists who took advantage of those less able to care for themselves. Women, and especially street kids, were there to be ignored, but the women were to be used as well and by as many men as there were around at the time, mostly drunks the lot of them, all down-and-outers most likely.

El Cuartel was such an example of some of these images. My mother was not a prisoner and neither was I, but the soldiers used her freely and with no consequence to themselves as the poor soul, my mom, had to succumb to their needs. I, on the other hand, had a good time because I was being fed and had kids to play with. I didn't have to fight to defend my mom because she was getting some of the things that she needed and wanted: she had something to drink, her child was getting fed, and she was able to watch over me. God bless her soul.

Two Insignificant People Living Insignificant Lives

1920 photograph of Avenida Tercera (3rd Avenue) in Agua Prieta. Note the several street kids, some of which may have been living a life similar to my father. Courtesy of mexicoenfotos.com/centli.

Agua Prieta Plaza Jose Azueta with gazebo and Catholic Church, 1945. My wife Patty and I visited this park during our tour; it looks quite similar today though with larger trees and newer facilities. Courtesy of mexicoenfotos.com/yayozarate.

Early time period public domain postcard image of (Main Street) G Avenue, Douglas, Arizona, most likely before my father was born in 1922 given the production years of the automobiles. Based on my research his mother, Guadalupe, could have been living in Douglas around this time.

The Sunset G Avenue Grocery Store was located on the first floor of the two-story Samson Hotel to the far right; it's now a vacant lot. I believe Trinidad Islava was employed at this grocery store location during the mid to late 1920s as documented in the Douglas telephone directories of the time, and as stated by my father's recollection. The third dark building was called Whimpy's, a hamburger joint; it's also now a vacant lot. Only the first two buildings from left to right remain today. The proprietor, Robin, owner/operator of this business now called The Avenue Hotel Bed and Breakfast, graciously texted me a copy of and permission to use this photograph that hangs in the lobby.

El Cuartel location with some remaining buildings. There are brick building extensions to the rear, but there were so many vehicles and some junk scattered about that those pictures were not included. I believe that the higher, second facility could possibly be from the time period of my father's writings, given the larger, open interior spaces that would lend themselves to horse stables. Photo courtesy of my wife, Patty, during our visit.

CHAPTER SIX

Prohibition was enacted in the United States in 1919 and was in effect until 1933. As a consequence, a lot of Americans traveled to Mexico to do their drinking in Agua Prieta where most of my young years were spent. I remember times when the American gringos, as they were called, came to the cantinas riding their horses and ready to do some serious drinking. There were horse tie rails made out of unfinished wooden posts in front of the cantinas. When the gringos came to drink, I, like other kids, rushed to get the job of watching their horses, and we would get paid for that, maybe a penny or two (Indian head pennies), sometimes as much as a nickel.

At one time during Prohibition I lived with a family in Agua Prieta; however, I have no recollection of how I came to live there. This particular family consisted of the mother and two sons. I forget their names except for the one son who was an emaciated, ulcerated, sickly, grouchy bastard. His name was Miguel. He took a dislike to me because I was a kid off the streets and his mother and brother liked me. They both got on Miguel's ass when he got mean and ugly with me. I don't know how long I stayed there, or as I said, even how I came to be there, except that this was not an ordinary home. This was a house of ill repute that catered exclusively to Americans who needed a place to drink and desired to purchase a woman for their pleasures. The men who frequented this brothel had money and could well afford to pay for everything that they wanted. These men came in big, fancy cars.

This was no ordinary whorehouse, as it had a huge parlor and bar, which was tended by the other son of the madam and was a gold mine to them. The location was not too far from El Cuartel, and was set in a very nice yard behind a wrought iron fence. The house had a front porch, next to which was a long driveway to the back of the facilities. The driveway had a high adobe fence on one side and the house on the other. In the back was an outbuilding with a garage and a room upstairs that well might have been where I slept.

At the rear area between the outbuilding and the house, there was what had been at one time a carriage storage facility. In this unused area were remnants of old wagons, wheels, horse collars, reins, and other tack items. On the walls of this storage place were also some car tire wheels, the solid ones. It was behind these tire rims that I used to hide the little reflector license plate holder buttons that I stole from the big, nice American cars that came to visit the brothel. I must have stolen dozens of these pretty reflectors, red, green, blue, yellow, and white. These reflectors had a wing nut that came with them to hold the license plates in place. There were usually four to a plate, but I never took off all four because the plate would fall off. I had no use for these little glass buttons except that I thought they were colorful. Whoever moved those tire wheels after I no longer lived there must have been quite surprised with my personal treasure!

It was a comfortable stay at this brothel except for Miguel, but

I stayed away from the bastard. I ate at the house, ate well too, but I had to eat while Miguel was taking a nap because he really had a hard time with my infringing on his privacy. While there, I also had a job, an honest-to-goodness job. The lady of the house was a madam and had several girls working for her, mostly young, pretty Mexican girls for the rich Americans, referred to by the girls mostly as *"los gringos."* My job was to pick up the soiled towels from the girls working in the brothel, take the towels to the laundry, and bring back clean ones. The girls used to cuddle me and tease me about how someday I would grow up and be able to do what the big boys did to girls. They would also pay me a little, maybe *cinco centavos* (five Mexican pennies), sometimes a little more. But as always, my mother came and found out where I was and I had to go.

As of yet in this accounting of my early years, I haven't mentioned in any detail my being scared. Yes, I was scared many times when I was with my mom, especially when she was intoxicated. Mom could be on a binge for weeks and lose track of me, but eventually she would find me and I was always afraid of her because I didn't know what she was going to do, or if we were going some other place. But then again, I was happy she was alive and as well as could be expected. Nonetheless, when this was the case, she would be very firm with me, and I had to do what she wanted or she would beat up on me. I don't know why, maybe because she didn't know where I had been at the time.

My mother and I must have been quite a sight. Here was a woman, obviously drunk, pulling a sobbing kid, maybe hungry or sick, surely scared, and in my heart embarrassed for the both of us. And of course, some kids made fun of us. Because of our perpetual wanderings, my mother and I were almost always in the same areas or neighborhoods in and around Agua Prieta; we were probably a common sight. My mom and I, neither one of us a pretty picture, both unclean, shabbily dressed, and going no place in particular. Some of the same people that would see us as a drunken woman and a helpless little guy, most likely fed me and maybe put me up for the night at some time. I can still hear the mothers scolding the kids because they would make fun and laugh at the spectacle of my mother and me. There is probably nothing more demeaning to a kid than a parent that creates an embarrassment to the family. So I was thinking in my little mind, "Mother we are looking bad and I wish you wouldn't drink," and I am also thinking, "Mother, I am hungry, tired and I am angry at you because you are not like other mothers." I have to believe that as a young kid who survived amidst all the iniquities, I matured mentally beyond my years. I was only nine or ten years old, maybe younger, certainly not much older.

Life could not have been all mean and ugly all of the time. For me there had to have been some happy days and weeks. No matter how bad some things got, or for how long, a short space of good things could heal those sad times. God forbid that all I would get were bad things. What a terrible person one could turn out to be.

One such good experience was the time that I stayed with a family for maybe a week or a month, a nice family that took pity on me and took care of me, a poor family but a stable one. I was provided clean clothes and had other kids to play with me. This family had milk delivered to their door every day and the milkman had a horse-pulled wagon, a funny little wagon with canvas sides that the milkman rolled up so people could come and buy cheese, milk, and other dairy products. The horse that pulled the wagon had a head plumage just to be fancy; the wagon was painted white.

The milkman would walk from house to house delivering milk, which he sold by the litro, liter. The woman of the house where I was staying would go to the door with a pan and the milkman would pour the milk into this pan and she would pay him. We kids would watch the milkman go from door to door, and when he got some distance away from the wagon, he would whistle and the horse would come to catch up with him. That was the highlight of the day. The milkman would whistle like I still do when I want to get my sons' attention. My family all knew my whistle that I learned from the milkman. What a joy!

The Santa who never came is an example of one of my hopeful but sad recollections. What brought this to mind was the other day during December I went to SouthCenter located in Tukwila, Washington, where my wife, Joan, and I presently live. As I was walking in the mall, I noticed a booth that had a sign about Christmas. On the booth there were a couple of boxes filled with cards. These cards had names of underprivileged kids with their requests for something that they wished for Christmas. I picked out a card and the name was Tim, seven years old, size ten. He wanted a Dallas Cowboy jersey, and I thought for a minute that here was a little boy wishing for something and I could make that wish come true. And I did.

When I was a little boy living in Mexico, I had heard a lot of stories about Santo Claus who always left toys for kids. On Christmas Eve he had reindeer that pulled his sleigh across the sky on his way to visit little children with gifts to give them. And, he always came at night, late at night. I really don't know how many years I looked for this Santo Claus to come, but picture this poor little kid, more than likely sleeping in somebody else's house, and with a cheek on a cold window, waiting to hear the little bells that Santo

Claus's reindeer wore, running across the sky with a fat little man hauling a big bag full of toys, and I was sure one was for me. He never came, but that was not so hard to take because the poor families that I stayed with, even if they had kids, Santo would forget them too.

As long as I live, Christmas will always bring that picture to mind of me waiting for the Santo Claus who never arrives. I always made sure that my children never had to be without presents and a tree. Janet, my first wife and our children's mother, and I would always decorate the Christmas tree and on Christmas Eve put all the toys under it after the kids went to bed. It was always a long night for Janet and me, but in the morning the pleasure of seeing the faces of our children was worth all the hard work!

THE VERGARA FAMILY PHOTOGRAPHS

Antonio Vergara and his second wife, Margarita Garcia, wedding day photo, April 20, 1908. Photo from my father's personal family collection.

Two Insignificant People Living Insignificant Lives

Antonio Vergara family including his four daughters born with Clotilde, his first wife. On far left is second born, Trini, then Magdalena the oldest, second wife Margarita, Antonio, next person I believe is Margarita's sister Catilena, then third born Gilda, who apparently died early in life, and youngest, Guadalupe, my father's mother. Date of photograph estimated at 1910; from Vergara family photo collection.

Margarita Vergara with, I believe, her daughter Amalia. Photo location is most likely the 1250 6th Avenue, Tucson address and taken in the later 1930s prior to Margarita's death. Photo from the Vergara Family.

Two Insignificant People Living Insignificant Lives

Margarita Vergara with four of the five children she had with Antonio Vergara during his second marriage. His first wife, Clotilde Vergara, died in 1906. All of the children from this second marriage are, eventually, my father's future aunts and uncles as they are all half brothers and sisters to Guadalupe, my dad's mom. The oldest child, Emma, born in 1910, is on the top left, with Amalia (third child), Antonio Jr. (second child), Alberto (fourth child), and mother Margarita. My dad's Uncle Bobby was the fifth child born in 1919. Photo from the Vergara family.

Two for You, One for Me

On the left is Rudy Islava, son of Trinidad Islava, brother of Clotilde, the first wife of Antonio Vergara Sr. Next to him is Antonio Vergara Jr. Date of family photo is unknown. Dad's personal photo album.

On the left is Roberto Vergara with older brother Alberto; date and location of photo unknown. Roberto, or as my dad called him for the rest of both of their lives "Uncle Bobby," were lifelong friends and more like brothers. Later in the narrative of my father's story the Vergara second family becomes a more significant part of his life. Vergara family photo.

IMAGES OF THE CITIES AND TOWNS ROUTINELY VISITED

Bird's-eye vista of Hermosillo. Early twentieth century photograph. Courtesy of mexicoenfotos/centli.

Period photograph of Plaza De Armas, Hermosillo, the city park with gazebo. Most likely my father and his mother rested here at some time during their various trips to Hermosillo. Courtesy of mexicoenfotos/centli.

Two Insignificant People Living Insignificant Lives

1910–1930 foothills and mountain living and a good view of Cananea, Sonora, Mexico. It's a given that my father and his mother walked these dirt roads both into and out of Cananea. Photo courtesy of mexicoenfotos/yayozarate.

Period postcard showing vista of Cananea. Image includes railroad trestle that served the copper smelter, a major employer. Courtesy of mexicoenfotos/centli.

*Period photo of Cananea street life where, perhaps, one day my father rested out of the sun while searching for his mom.
Courtesy mexicoenfotos/centli.*

This time period photo shows the international line (slightly diagonal from upper left center to lower right center) separating Nogales, Sonora, Mexico, on the right, and Nogales, Arizona, on the left. The center cross street left to right is the main north/south road to formally cross between countries. Note the small administrative buildings opposite one another. I suspect that my father and his mother were familiar with crossing at this location when doing so legally. Through Ancestry.com I found documentation of several early twentieth century crossings by all of the first Vergara family except for his first wife, Clotilde. After she passed in 1906, her siblings took a significant role in the lives of the four Vergara sisters as many times the girls were met at this crossing by Islava family members.
Courtesy of mexicoenfotos/centli.

Antonio Vergara, for a short period of time in 1925, operated a bar in Nogales called "Mi Officina," located on the above Calle Elias Street. The husbands of his daughters Magdalena and Trini were bartenders that apparently drank up a good part of the profits and the bar closed after three months. Photo courtesy of mexicoenfotos/centli.

Panorama period postcard of Nogales, Mexico; note the city park and gazebo so typical of Mexican cities and towns. In all likelihood my father and grandmother spent some time in this city park during their wanderings to both Nogales border towns. When visiting here they would most likely go to visit his aunt Magdalena, his mother Guadalupe's older sister. Photo courtesy mexicoenfotos/centli.

Period postcard of the public market in Nogales, Mexico. Not quite the same scale as the one in Hermosillo where my father found it easier to panhandle to passersby. Courtesy of mexicoenfotos/centli.

This scene represents some of the images that my father remembered seeing as to how some people traveled throughout the border towns from place to place. Courtesy www.apsoncezar.com.

1924 aerial photograph of border crossing at Naco, Arizona, and Naco, Mexico. There is a US Army installation in the foreground (lower center two squares and outbuildings) that was established during the Mexican Revolution to protect the border. The actual border crossing is at the center of longest, light color road, lower left to upper right, and railroad tracks from lower right to upper left. Note the dirt road leading southwesterly out of Naco toward Cananea and imagine my father and his mother walking, hitchhiking, or somehow traveling during their many wanderings. Around 1920 Antonio Vergara moved his second family to Naco, Arizona, and opened a butcher shop, which lasted for less than two years. It is unlikely any of the four daughters from his first family accompanied them to Naco, as they would have been twenty to twenty-six years old at that time, with my father's mother Guadalupe being the youngest. Photo courtesy of Fort Huachuca Museum.

Two Insignificant People Living Insignificant Lives

Naco border crossing; the white, hipped roof building right/center is the Mexican administrative facility. Photo taken from Naco, Mexico, toward Naco, Arizona. Courtesy of mexicoenfotos/centli.

Photo taken from Naco, Mexico, by the border fence looking toward the Naco, Arizona, border crossing administrative building. The Mexican admin building has several people sitting and standing out front. Courtesy of mexicoenfotos/yayozarate.

Time period Naco, Mexico, street scene. After Antonio Vergara's Naco, Arizona, butcher shop failed, he worked a short time for himself walking to the Arizona town of Huachuca thirty miles one way alongside a burro loaded with contraband mescal. He would barter for money, shoes, and coats that he would then take back to Naco with him and sell. His wife stayed in Naco with their children and also served as a midwife. Then in 1922 Antonio went to Tucson to begin working on the railroad, after which, he moved his family to Tucson and rented a house. Antonio saved his money, left the railroad job, and then purchased a pool hall located on Congress and Church streets in Tucson. In 1925 he sold it to a Japanese businessman. After living in Arizona for five years, he applied for United States citizenship. Courtesy of mexicoenfotos/yayozarate.

PART TWO

1934–1936

The Mendoza Family—A New Beginning

Contemporary Loretto School in Douglas, Arizona, visited by my wife and me during our trip. We lunched and toured the school with the Administrator, Sister Mary Francine, walking the same halls that my father did at the age of twelve until he was fourteen, starting school in the fourth or fifth grade. The vinyl flooring material and design, though very well maintained, seemed it could have been from the same period as my dad. Photographs taken by my wife, Patty.

CHAPTER SEVEN

This life phase is going to fit someplace in these writings as a pivotal part of my life. It's really the basis of knowing what it means to be able to say I know where home is, and I know that I'll eat and have a place to sleep. You can't imagine the peace of mind. Señor Miguel and Señora Maria Mendoza made a home for me that was really my first lasting experience of what it is to have a meaningful life, full of love, security, and caring. Imagine strangers all of a sudden change your life because they see a child in need. As you know by now, my mom and I frequented Agua Prieta, Sonora, Mexico, probably more than other border towns because it was more removed from family interference. She wanted to be totally independent of family involvement because she thought that they would want me to stay with them.

In Agua Prieta, right at the border crossing is the Immigration Building, an old brick building with an iron fence around it and lots of trees. All the people coming from Douglas to go shopping for groceries in Agua Prieta go by that building. At that time I was about twelve years old and an experienced boy of the streets. As a routine I had stood at this corner quite often because it was a place to pick up a handout, or in other words, panhandle. I had noticed this nice older man always coming to Mexico to do his shopping, and at times he would give me five cents or something and just talk a little. On his way home he would have his shopping bags and sometimes would give me an orange or a cookie in passing. This sort of became a way of meeting.

One day he asked me if I had been to Douglas, and I answered that on several occasions I had with my mom. Another time he asked me where I lived and I told him in Agua Prieta, but at no particular place. He asked about my mother. This was about 1934 or so and I was twelve and street-smart and this man, fortunately, was so sincere. He asked me if I would like to visit his house, told me he had a wife and a daughter Carlota, and an older daughter Maria, who had several kids, some about my age. I told him that going into the United States would be easy for me because I thought I was an American citizen, and that I had a relative who owned a store (that would be my mother's uncle Trinidad Islava), though at the time I did not know where the store was. He said that if I would come to Douglas with him I could stay at his house and that he would talk to his wife. I said OK but I was still afraid that my mother would find out where I was staying and would come and get me. I can see this kind man, wearing bib coveralls, a blue work shirt, a hat, and a blue jacket; he had a mustache and was short.

Another day, soon after our initial discussion of my living with him and his family, he asked me about my schooling and more about my mother. I explained the situation and he felt sorry for me. He said, "You carry one of the shopping bags and just let me do the talking to the border guy." Five minutes later I was in Douglas, no trouble. The days of spending nights alone, sleeping anyplace were over. I was a very good kid; I caused no trouble at all. I met

The Mendoza Family—A New Beginning

his grandkids; they lived next door. Maria, his wife, liked me. The younger daughter, Carlota, was seventeen or eighteen, I suppose; she treated me like family. I had my own room. Of course, I had to tell them everything about my mother, about not really going to school steadily. They contacted the welfare lady and I became a ward of the state. They bought my clothes and the state may have helped them financially, I don't know.

The Mendozas made it their business to see that I would adjust to a normal life as a family member. I, of course, was expected to do as a family member would do and carry my share of the load of being a complete family. For example, there was a huge smelter across from the railroad tracks in what was really a desert and maybe two or three miles away from their house. Miguel, Maria, the kids, and I would go to the vacant desert to gather firewood consisting of dead mesquite tree branches and different types of cactuses that provided wood for burning at home.

In Arizona the saguaro cactus are very prominent and we kids used to like to pick and eat the fruit from them. The fruit is located way up on the top and we used to throw rocks and sticks to knock them off, or use real long poles with wire to remove them. It was lots of work but fun, and the fruit was tasty. The other thing that we would eat off of plants and trees were the long beans of the mesquite tree. These long shells look like green beans and when they dry, they are very sweet. You can't swallow the bean—just the juice. Also, the flat cactuses with fruit on their tops are very prickly, but very sweet; you can eat the whole thing and they are called *nopal*, cactuses. My uncle Bobby had these in his backyard at the San Jose house when he lived there; son, you may remember seeing them there when we visited his family.

Miguel and Maria Mendoza enrolled me in Loretto Catholic

School in Douglas. As a coincidence, the Catholic church that they went to was the same Church of the Immaculate Conception that I had been baptized in several years before. While I was being indoctrinated into their family atmosphere, I had to do a lot of things that to me, a street kid, were very different, but I was very willing and able to adjust easily. For the first time I was required and expected to go to church and confession every Saturday, as well as saying prayers before every meal and the rosary every night, and having Holy Communion every time we went to church, which was very often.

I also had to attend catechism at the nuns' house, located close to the church, on Saturdays and other times when I had nothing to do. Through the Mendozas the nuns learned of my personal history and background, and I was provided the opportunity to help them around their home. I truly enjoyed helping the nuns with their huge garden: digging, weeding, planting, and harvesting, whatever I was asked to do. That whole episode with them in my life was a very meaningful learning experience for me. I learned that life could be rich and productive and that whatever I could contribute was worth a lot and appreciated. My most favorite part of working for them came on hot days when I was rewarded with a glass of cold milk and cookies that the nuns fed me under a most beautiful grape arbor that grew in their yard. Sometimes when I worked there all day, they fed me lunch too. The Mendozas were proud of me because the nuns always told them what a good worker I was. This did wonders for my self-esteem.

Eventually the nuns decided that I was such a fine lad that I should become an altar boy. My, was I proud to be that! I had to learn Latin. In the old days mass was said in Latin and the altar boys had to know all the responses and we got to ring the bells on the altar at certain times during the mass. The other thing that I really liked to do as an altar boy was when we had to pass the money basket around the pews. I was able to see all the pretty little girls sitting with their folks and smiling and making eyes at me in my long, white altar boy gown. I was so proud!

Father Ramos and Father Healy (I can't for the life of me imagine how I can remember these Fathers' names) were my direction to a good and honest life. They also taught me respect and discipline. Along with the Mendozas and the nuns, these were the various influences that together changed my life. And, I guess, that somehow I've always known right from wrong. But still, in my life I have done some things that were not always right; never anything serious or damaging to people or property because I was always afraid of the consequences.

Going to Catholic school was also a unique experience. I was old for the school grades that I was attending during 1934. I was placed possibly in the fourth or fifth grade, though I had infrequently attended school in Sonora, Mexico, but never continually. I don't believe that I could put together a school attendance of two to three months straight; I just can't. There was nobody to make me go to school or get me ready to go; we had no home base and in Sonora, I believe nobody cared what you did. If I attended school, it had to be a day here and two days there. When I stayed with compassionate families that had kids who went to school, I guess I tagged along. For me that is probably the saddest part of my life, my lack of education.

Miguel and Maria Mendoza had two daughters who I mentioned before, Carlota and Maria. Carlota was at home; Maria lived next door with her husband, Ricardo Millan, and their three kids. Their children all went to public school, I guess. I don't really know why I went to Catholic school; that's what the Mendozas thought I needed. Carlota helped me with schoolwork as she knew that I couldn't speak English or read. Spanish was all I knew; she taught me one way or another. Somehow I've always been able to memorize things. I've been blessed with a good learning capability. When I lived with the Mendozas, they kept me active doing things that are expected of family members, chores that contribute to the family function. The Mendozas were poor in general, as were a lot of households in the United States during the Depression. I believe that Miguel and Ricardo Millan both worked with the federal program at the time called Works Progress Administration, making about a dollar per day. But in family values and wonderful, helpful guidance, the Mendozas were rich beyond belief.

My second wife, Joan, and I visited the Church of the Immaculate Conception in Douglas when we took the previously mentioned 1984 trip to Arizona along with my uncle Bobby and his wife, Mary; the city still looks the same. From the Mendozas' house to the church it was a long walk and I would always take a shortcut through a city park. I remember the walk so well because on the way to the church I had to pass by the mulberry trees, which were bearing fruit. The fruit was so sweet, juicy, and very purple and left a terrific stain on your hands, mouth, clothes, and shoes. Maria Mendoza made the most tasty pies with these berries. When I revisited the place in 1984, the trees had been cut down because, I suppose, over the years the sidewalks were so terribly stained. Fun memories for me though.

The walks to work at the nuns' gardens provided me with memories that to this day are fresh. Walking home one day (it's nice to be able to say going home because the Mendozas' home was my home), I passed a little Model A delivery truck. This was a Milky

Way candy man's truck with glass windows so I could see the shelves with boxes and boxes of Milky Ways—yummy chocolate candy bars. I had to press my face against the glass windows to get a closer look and could almost taste the chocolate. I had never had a Milky Way candy, so I didn't know what they tasted like, but I knew that if I ever could buy a candy bar, it would have to be a Milky Way!

My most memorable little church-to-home experience is one day after the Fourth of July while I was walking my favorite route home. I was kicking little rocks, cans, sticks, empty paper bags, just to break the monotony of walking; it was good entertainment but hard on shoes. I kicked a cardboard tube that the day before had been a rocket, I guess. I tried to look through it but couldn't, so I took it home. I imagined that there must be some powder that had not burned. So I went to the backyard, dropped a match in one end, and lowered the other end with my bare hand. I guess I didn't want the fire to escape. I suppose that there wasn't a lot of powder, but what was there exploded and all the fire came out where my bare hand was covering the end of the cardboard tube. Wow, what a painful burn! The Mendozas were all excited and concerned because I had burned myself, so they thought of a cure. This "medicine" was to put lard on the burn and then to hold my hand over a hot stove. Hurt like hell, but lo and behold it healed and it never scarred; they sure knew what they were doing.

One routine chore that I had at home that I most looked forward to was roasting coffee beans. Miguel Mendoza would buy the coffee beans in Mexico as it was cheaper there; at that time the exchange rate I believe was still two pesos to the dollar. Anyway, it was my job to roast the coffee. Wow, that was neat and most aromatic! As the coffee roasted, I put in sugar and blended it in by stirring. When it was roasted and cooled, it was my job to grind it in the small hand grinder—such wonderful smells. Maria always made it a point to fuss over what a good job I had done. She said in Spanish, "Ricardo eres un muchachito muy bueno." This means Ricardo, you are a very nice little boy. Can you imagine what that did for me to get hugged and told what a good boy I was?

So many things come to mind, some of no consequence but still part of living with the Mendozas. When I used to go to work at the nuns' house, it was a lot of labor but also a lot of fun. There was a house adjoining the nuns' big yard, a beautiful big brick house with well-kept grounds. At that house lived an older lady. Her husband had been a doctor and she hired a Hispanic man that took care of her home maintenance needs, and was also her chauffeur. She had an old Buick sedan that he washed and waxed. Well, he would observe me as I worked in the nuns' yard; his name was Rubio. One day he asked me if I would care to help him and do the same thing I was doing for the nuns. I said I would, so when I went home I told Miguel and Maria that I had a job doing work at the doctor's house and getting paid. I believe I got a dollar a day and soup and sandwiches. Also, sometimes I could help Rubio wax the fancy Buick. After I had worked for a while doing lawns and learning how to use the yard tools, I thought I could make a little more money by doing other peoples' yards.

I was thinking about one particular time when I first started knocking on doors where I thought there might be a chance for doing some yard work, as the place looked like it needed some help. Mind you my English was still a big mystery to me. I had just started going to school and at the Mendozas' we always spoke Spanish. Some or most of the doors I knocked on were where people lived who looked like they could pay for yard work, Americans,

English speaking of course. Here's a small Hispanic kid from across the tracks where poor people lived, asking for work. I had no tools for yard work but I thought they would have. I knocked, somebody answered, and I blurted out, "Could I kill your lawn?" They laughed. I wondered why as they asked how much money to clean the yard. I would say fifty cents; they took pity and gave me a job. I always did a good job. This was my life phase in learning when you work you get paid; I never to this day have forgotten that experience. I don't believe I did that for too long because I had to walk all the way past where the church and the nuns' residence were located in order to access the homes where the very rich people lived. And besides, I had jobs at both the nuns' and the doctor's homes. When I think about this now, probably nobody was rich but I thought they were since they all had cars and big clean homes.

The Depression years were really a time for learning to be poor and how to survive. Every dime I made I gave to the Mendozas; it wasn't much but they really appreciated it. They always would say I was a good boy and love me a little with a hug; boy, did that feel good! Being poor in those days meant going to the commissary where people lined up to get food, clothes, shoes, and other handouts. The Mendozas and I would line up and receive cheese, spam, canned corned beef, sugar, flour, beans, and other staples. We didn't get much but it was welcomed by all. At that time these commissaries played a major role in the National Recovery Act, a government welfare program.

My most favorite thing to get in the way of clothes from the commissary was a pair of jeans with bell bottoms. They had little snap buttons with a belt-like flap and the snap buttons looked neat. Also, the bell-bottom trousers had a red wedge that was sewn on the trouser legs to widen them at the bottom. Wow, they were really sharp and I felt so proud to wear them! After all, at twelve years old you want the girls to like you and to think how neat you looked in bell-bottom trousers.

My life with the Mendozas gave me many important, lasting values that to this day are still a part of me; this is where I learned family values. The church that to this day is important to me. A person needs a faith to hold on to. They taught me even when everything fails your God is always there; when nothing else is dependable, faith is. It doesn't mean that you are always good. Many mistakes I've made in life, though God will always forgive. When you get ill as I am with cancer, God is my strength. I haven't forgotten for one minute that for the Mendozas, church was their everything. Wow, I haven't since said more rosaries, attended more masses, said more prayers, or received more communions than when I lived with them.

They also taught me to appreciate work no matter how little you earned because it all helps. When I earned fifty cents and gave it to them, they hugged and held me and always told me sweet words of appreciation. They taught me cleanliness no matter how poor you are. If you are clean and have a tidy home, life appears much richer. Honesty was a virtue that I learned from them. No matter what the circumstances, honesty and not taking things that didn't belong to you was important. They knew what kind of life I'd lived and they wanted to teach me that there was a different and better way to live. My eyes tear a little when I think of all that I learned from them that shaped my adult life. May their souls rest in peace.

I suppose that I lived with the Mendozas for a little over two years, from sometime in 1934 to an unknown date in 1936 or later. After that, the state found out that I was a homeless boy prior to

The Mendoza Family—A New Beginning

residing in their home, or maybe they knew from the beginning of my living with the Mendozas. I just do not know. State agency representatives made efforts to locate any relatives who may exist because they knew by now that I had been born in Arizona and was a United States citizen. Till this day that part of my Mendoza family experience remains very vague in my memory. I just remember that all of a sudden I was getting ready to go to Tucson to live with my grandparents, Antonio and Margarita Vergara, and the state lady was buying me new clothes and shoes to wear when I was sent back to Tucson. I guess I was excited to be going there because I had temporarily lived with my grandparents in 1933, but my mother came and took me back with her. That was when I was eleven, and here it was 1936 or so.

I would love to remember all of how this transfer of life happened, but I've no recollection. However, I do remember being taken to the Douglas train station and all the Mendozas were there. I am sure we all hugged and cried and that was the way it all ended. I am sorry to say that at fourteen years of age, I was not really touched by all the emotion that had to be taking place at that moment. I am sure that I loved and respected them very much. They had taught me there was another way that people lived and existed as a family. I am today a product of their love and teachings. There is some sadness as I write this and it touches my heart to think of myself as being almost a little bit ungrateful. But I really wasn't; I was just calloused to things changing. All my life had been uncertain and this was just another reminder to once again brace myself. God Bless the Mendozas!

A son's notes of explanation: My research with the State of Arizona Family Services turned up no records of my father and the Mendoza family, in part because the state data system for such records was minimal at best at that time, and damaging fires and misplacement during relocation of records and/or facilities took their toll. In addition, there is a lapse in my father's recollections for the next two plus years of his life upon coming home from living with the Mendozas. When I questioned him concerning this lapse, he seemed to indicate that his memory of events was either nonexistent or irrelevant to his personal effort to write what was important to him. I did not press the matter, though one can certainly conclude from his writing that it was during this period of time that my father's relationships began with his pals Frank Hughes, Ernie Acuña, and Tony Hernández. These friendships continued to grow over time to become meaningful and enduring, and play a significant role in Dad's Civilian Conservation Corps experience and, with the exception of Tony Hernández, Dad's early army boot camp memories as his life story continues to unfold.

The Mendoza Family—A New Beginning

The postcard photo, c. 1945, provides the opposite view of the border image in Chapter 2. In fact, that photo was most likely taken from this Mexican border facility roof while standing next to the right of the central tower looking toward the US border facilities. My father would panhandle at the corner directly behind the auto at the center pole. Courtesy of mexicoenfotos/yayozarate.

An earlier twentieth century postcard photograph of the Phelps Dodge Copper Queen Smelter in the desert mentioned by my father. This smelter was the economic cornerstone of Douglas, Arizona; the city is still trying to recover subsequent to the smelter's closure in 1987 due to environmental issues. Courtesy of Pomona Public Library; The Francher Foto Postcard Collection; Public Domain.

Today's Immaculate Conception Church, Douglas, Arizona. My father was baptized at and reintroduced to this church by the Mendoza family. My wife and I met a kind lady in front of the church who directed us to go just down the street to the location of the nun's residence where my father worked for them during his stay with the Mendoza family. After listening to our purpose of being in Douglas, she mentioned that her parents used to play cards with Father Healy, a priest that had a favorable life influence on my father. Photo courtesy of my wife, Patty.

The Mendoza Family—A New Beginning

Two nuns, Sisters Lucy and Helen, Sisters of Notre Dame, now occupy this residence, which is leased from the House of the Company of Mary, the original order of nuns occupying the home when my father worked for them at this location. My wife and I had a great visit discussing my father's story and being given a tour of the home and grounds. During our visit we learned that the residence was originally owned by the Burdett Packard family, one of the founding families of Douglas. He donated this home to the Order of the House of the Company of Mary, currently located in Tustin, California. The grounds around the home are now changed, of course, including the location for a preschool sited behind this view of the house, the grape arbor long gone now. This photo is taken from a residential side street, and the porch above curves around to the front entrance to the right, off of East 10th St.; too many trees to see the front of the house in a photograph. This photo courtesy of my wife, Patty.

Reverend Bernard Healy on the left helped to put my father's life on a proper course and remained a lasting influence on him. Reverend Healy also signed what was likely a replacement of my father's original baptismal certificate that was dated late 1937. Most likely the original from 1922 was either lost or misplaced due to the homelessness of my father and his mother. Courtesy of Archdiocese of Tucson.

This postcard is most likely later than my father's time there and comes from a collection of historical images of Douglas, Arizona, and Agua Prieta, Mexico. However, this is definitely the city park that Dad would walk through as a shortcut to the Church of the Immaculate Conception. My wife and I visited the park during our stay in Douglas, Arizona. Courtesy of www.apsoncezar.com.

The Mendoza Family—A New Beginning

Time period post card of the El Paso and Southwestern Railroad Douglas Train Depot built in 1913. Public Domain.

PART THREE

APRIL 1939–
SEPTEMBER 1940

The Civilian Conservation Corps—
Discipline, Responsibility, Manhood

Richard at seventeen, early December 1939 on a family visit from the CCC camp. This photo is believed to have been taken on the back porch at his grandparents' home in Tucson, located at 1250 South 6th Avenue. The site is now a parking lot that's close to the Santa Cruz Catholic Church. Photo is from Dad's personal collection and was unknown to me until after my father passed. It was given to me, among other familiar photos and documents belonging to Dad, by his wife, Joan. I had to have the image digitally improved and enlarged as my "original" was quite small.

CHAPTER EIGHT

A son's background for the reader: President Franklin D. Roosevelt's New Deal Program was created in the 1930s during the Great Depression in order to put the country's many unemployed people back to work. This was to be accomplished, hopefully, through restarting the national economy by redirecting our failed federal fiscal policies at that time. One of these public work programs was the establishment of the Civilian Conservation Corps (CCC) that targeted unemployed and/or married men from ages seventeen to late twenties/early thirties. Each state had the opportunity to plan, organize, administer, and implement these work programs that were managed at the delivery level using a military model with service personnel resources. Men were provided with rigid daily work objectives, lived with crewmates in camp settings exclusively in the work environment, and were expected to meet the demands for responsible personal and collective behavior and commitment. These programs were quite similar throughout the country, with the differences being driven primarily by the particular topographical, geographical, and environmental conditions and resources of any given state. The work was primarily hard, physical labor done out-of-doors in the forestlands and national parks, arid desert lands, waterways and river systems, rural areas, and small hamlets. For example, the work was varied and could include establishing forest recreational trail systems, campsites, and outbuildings; fencing of public lands; creating road access for difficult-to-reach locations; controlling soil erosion; and building bridges, just to name a few. The men received a small income, most of which was required to be sent home to families and/or loved ones. Here is Dad continuing on . . .

With the availability in Arizona of this new public work opportunity, in early April of 1939, after some discussion amongst ourselves, my buddies Frank Hughes, Ernie Acuña, Tony Hernández, and I joined the Civilian Conservation Corps in order to have something to do. We were frustrated with the fact that at that time there was a shortage of work. The Depression, of course, remained strongly felt and we were restless kids. My friends and I were all set to do something that had a decent purpose, and besides we would be together having fun with other kids our own age, or even a little bit older. Most importantly, all of us wanted and needed to make some income even though we would only be paid thirty dollars each per month. Our families benefited most since all workers were required to send home a majority of each paycheck, leaving us each with a small amount of money for sundries and pocket change.

At this time in our lives we were typical teenagers, never wild enough to get into trouble with the law, however. Drinking a little once in a while was OK, as was chasing the ladies in our spare time. In those days chasing girls didn't mean we would make out; we just received the pleasure of their company. Above all, for me, school was not the most important thing to do. By now, with the exception of my time spent with the Mendozas,

The Civilian Conservation Corps

you know that schooling had not been something that I did very well as it had never been a routine part of my life. As for my friends, I don't recall their schooling histories in any detail.

The four of us went to the CCC recruiting station in Tucson and asked if we could join and be sent to the same place. The officer said yes, then he asked us if we had had any trouble with the law and why we wanted to join. We all said no to the law question, then we each explained why we wanted to join the CCC—that we all needed money and our folks could use the little help we could provide by sending them most of our earnings. They next asked us if we had any serious medical problems, tuberculosis (TB), or any other illnesses. At that time TB was a very common thing to have, especially within the poorer populations. Each of us was fine in that regard. Some other restrictions included an age requirement of sixteen years old; I was just four months away from being seventeen. You also had to be of a certain height and weigh at least 130 pounds. They then gave us a quick health check because you had to be able to work. It was hard work and they expected you to be strong enough to do it; if you were sickly, they didn't want you.

My friends and I all passed the exam and then the weigh-in was next. Everyone lined up and purposely I lined up last. The guys came through just fine but I only weighed 110 pounds. "Well," the man says, "you are short twenty pounds." So I pleaded with the corporal who was doing the recruiting. I said my friends all passed and that I really wanted to go into the CCC camps and that I knew I would be able to do the work. My friends also put in their two cents worth of pleading and stating it would be nice if we could all go in together. The corporal stated that it looked like this was very important for all of us. He said, "I tell you what to do. Go buy about one dozen bananas and a quart of milk and eat them as fast as you can, drink all the milk, and then come right back and see what happens. I believe that you'll make the weight." I said, "Sure. I'll do it!"

My friends and I were committed to make this happen. We all pitched in our pocket change, maybe twenty-five cents, and walked to a store close by and purchased the bananas and quart of milk. There was a city park near the store, so we walked to it and all sat down. Of course, all of my friends were giving me words of encouragement. It took a little while to eat a dozen bananas and drink a quart of milk. The guys were laughing and making jokes and urging me on. I probably took forty-five minutes to do all that gorging, and then we had to walk back to the recruiting office. Thankfully, it wasn't very far to go. All the way back to the recruiting office the guys kept teasing me about how fat I looked and that I should easily make the weight requirement. Of course, all the joking and teasing was done in Spanish and we were all having a good time. Somehow in Spanish, it all seemed funnier, hardy laughs and all the screwing around.

When we got back to the recruiting office, the same guy that had weighed me before and had made the weight-increase suggestion said, "Well, how were the bananas?" All my friends started to laugh because they said to the corporal, "He loved the bananas and don't you think he looks fatter?" So he put me on the scale and everybody had to crowd around to see how I did. "Well" said the corporal, "you weigh one hundred twenty-seven and a half pounds. You can go with your buddies." Of course, they all laughed and said, "We told you you looked fatter!" So the entrance papers were signed and I was eligible to join the CCC. My grandmother, Margarita, had to make the final approval, which she did, so I reported the next day and off we all went to Buckeye, Arizona. (From my father's CCC service records this camp was formally referred to as G-109, Company 847, opening in October 7, 1938.) Though we didn't know it, we were to spend our time building what seemed like miles of fencing.

The CCC provided a train from Tucson to Phoenix, and we were picked up by an army truck and traveled the sixty miles to Buckeye, Arizona. They also saw to it that we had something to eat. My friends and I were in a group of several young men, all full of wonder as to what to expect. The CCC camps were quite regimented as they were administered by army personnel and officers. Discipline was the order of the day. I had no trouble with that. Well, the sixty miles to Buckeye was a hell of a long ride. Sixty miles in those days in an army truck was slow, bumpy, and boring. Some of the ride took us through the desert, maybe fifteen miles. When we arrived at Buckeye, we saw that it was just a wide spot in the road with a service station and country store next to a small tavern. Not much clientele. There was also a small post office in the general store. The truck proceeded out of Buckeye on a desert road the final miles. My friends and I were excited to get to where we were going as we were anticipating a lot of different things, including hard work, fun experiences, and raising a little hell now that we were away from home and on our own—all part of growing up and learning lots of new things.

Finally we arrived at the camp. We were all a little dusty and thirsty but excited to be at the place that was going to be our home for some time. The sergeant told us to fall out and line up behind the truck. He called our names and we answered yeah. After the roll call he marched us to a wooden building that was the supply room and advised us that we were going to be issued our clothing and necessary equipment to be officially in the CCC. Our clothing issue was simple and it took very little time. We were loaded with everything and then marched to our barracks, where we picked out our beds. The mattresses were rolled up and there were clean sheets, blankets, pillows, pillowcases, and a footlocker to place all of your clothes into. In addition, we had a standing wooden closet in which to place our work clothes and such. I felt pretty good; everything here belonged to me.

Then there was the corporal in charge of the barracks. He taught us how to make the beds and explained exactly how they were to be made. If they did not pass his inspection, he would tear it up and have you remake it. Discipline! It had been a long day and we were feeling the pressure. He said that dinner would be soon and to clean up for it. By this time all the work crews that had been in the field started coming in and, of course, making all the remarks that go on, making fun of the new recruits. They started asking how the girls were back home and how we would have to go without them as there were no girls here except at payday. It was a lot of idle conversation and comedy. At dinner all the new recruits were put on different tables, probably because we had not yet had our final medical exams and our shots. Anyway, what a meal I had! Never had I seen so much food in one place before, platters and platters of food. Each table had a waiter, and if he thought we needed more refills, he took care of it. We all thought, "WOW!"

After dinner we just goofed around, getting used to our new quarters, putting stuff away, making our beds, and laughing because we just knew that making a bed was not a very simple job. I personally did not want to have my bed torn up and have to remake it, so we all teased each other. All of the new recruits were placed in the same section. The one thing that I just happen to remember: there were no black kids in our camp. I don't know why, segregation, I guess. But that was the way things were then; the schools in Arizona were all segregated. Lights went out at ten o'clock and it was sack time. All the new recruits were reminded that we would be awakened in the morning by someone coming through the barracks with a bell that meant we had to be up and ready to go to breakfast in thirty minutes. We were to have our beds made and ourselves cleaned up, and be dressed in our new fatigues and work shoes. All the new recruits were to stay in camp for shots, exams, and some training classes.

Day one of the CCC camp life, what a breakfast! Things I had never seen before, French toast, ham, all kinds of eggs fried or scrambled, dry cereal, all the milk you could drink; there was such excitement over food and it was well prepared. I thought it was great! After breakfast the sergeant said to go back to the barracks and wait until we were called out and then we would be going to the infirmary. They would then give us our final examinations and shots. A little later the whistle blew and we fell in and the sergeant called the roll and told us that over the next couple of hours we would be processed and have all our exams finished. Then we would view some training films and receive orientation about what we needed to know to function as camp personnel. Remember that all the instructions now were in English. I had to concentrate on listening and understanding what was being said as they did not want to repeat it too many times, so my friends and I helped each other.

Exam time came and here we go again. We entered the infirmary and sat down waiting for our names to be called out so that we could receive our shots and redo some of the things we had done before in Tucson. Except this time it was the real final check-up. Everything checked out OK, breathing, heart, balls, no hernias. Then he said, "Now for the weight. Well, let's see, get on the scale and you weigh, according to this report, one hundred twenty-seven and a half pounds." He fiddled with the scale and he said, "There's something wrong here. It says you weigh one hundred ten pounds. They must have made an error in Tucson when they weighed you." Then the guys started to laugh because we had all thought, "Hell, if I weighed one hundred twenty-seven and a half pounds yesterday, certainly today should be the same." Then they told the nurse what I had done to meet the weight requirement. He laughed and said, "You'll have to put some meat on those bones. You're healthy and strong and we'll put some muscle on you." It was a beginning of a new life for me!

Next we went to some camp-life orientation. Cleanliness was number one, including personal hygiene, haircuts, and clean clothes; fortunately the laundry was done for us. However, all personnel had to iron their own clothes and shine their shoes, and the brass buttons on coats and jackets had to be polished bright. All our dress clothes and work clothes were army issue. Each person still had whatever civilian clothes one had when arriving at camp and it was OK to wear them when on liberty going to town. During the orientation there were many things we had to know, including the fact that discipline was paramount and standard procedure. Toward the end of the presentation we were informed that all of us would soon be allowed to go to town. Other than Buckeye there was another town to go to that was a little larger and had more opportunities to get into trouble. All personnel were informed that getting into trouble was not the thing to do as we had to make a good impression so people would welcome us. Throughout the orientation we were advised as to what to do and what not to do.

Next the new recruits were given the opportunity to do some little jobs; the sergeant broke us in quickly. The first thing that we learned was the word *policing up*, which meant camp cleanliness. The sergeant said that each of us would know that where we lived was not a pigpen, and that today when we broke for detail, we were to police up the camp area and "all I want to see are ass-holes and elbows. Pick up cigarette butts, chewing gum wrappers, and all the debris." My friends and I thought policing up was fun because the sergeant seemed to enjoy seeing all the recruits being very serious about our duties, especially since the camp area was large and there were lots of things to pick up. We all hoped that our experience would only get better.

After a few days all of us seemed to be getting a little used to the new routine, including all one wanted to eat, fantastic meals, and new friends from all over New Mexico, Texas, Colorado, and Arizona. Most of the fellows were younger, some were in their twenties, some early thirties; the youngest guys hung together, and the older guys did the same. There must have been 150 men in the camp, with army staff being the leaders and our observers.

Each morning the camp had reveille, and we saluted the flag and lined up for inspection, all very organized. After our breakfast we picked up tasty sack lunches, and it was then time to go to work. The men would meet at our assigned truck and off we went in all different directions. Some were to build miles and miles of barbed wire fences, digging by hand with a post-hole digger, putting up the fence posts. Other details would string the barbed wire, stretching it taut and nailing it to the posts. These fences were to keep cattle in where they belonged. Lifting and working with rolls of barbed wire put some muscle on everybody, and during the heat of the day we would take off our fatigue jackets and soak up sun. We thought we were really something and maybe that was true.

Work crews also dug dams. That particular task was accomplished with bulldozers and other heavy equipment, all operated by army personnel. There was a lot of shovel work too. It was all good, hard, clean, sweaty work that they expected us to do at a steady pace without killing ourselves, though there were schedules to maintain. The dams we built had a very good purpose where there was no water. These dams were large and deep because when it rains in the desert, flash flooding occurs and water just runs wild. This wild water forms rivers where there are no rivers and the dams would provide a means to capture this water and save it for the cattle, while at the same time, controlling desert erosion damage.

The work details consisted of ten to fifteen men, depending upon what we were planning to do that particular day. A crew might be way out in the desert someplace, maybe a couple of hours away from camp, maybe closer. There was a little screwing around once in a while. The same men were not always together and a mix of new ones meant different mischief. At lunchtime we would seek some shade to keep cool; though there is not too much shade provided in the sagebrush. Mesquite trees sometimes had shady areas. Men would nap and rest, and sometimes the older guys would smoke marijuana, joke, laugh, and screw around. I could never get interested in smoking marijuana; I was too chicken, I guess. Those fellows that did smoke it thought everything was funny. Finally, the lead man would get us up and started on the job again. At times when you stop and look at what we'd done, you could see this long, long line of posts and bright shiny wire going forever. And you would ask yourself, "Did we do that?" There was a lot more good to be found here than walking the streets back home.

We were paid thirty dollars a month and I had an allotment of twenty-two dollars initially sent home to my grandmother and she told me how much she appreciated the money. After she passed, I then sent the same amount to Aunt Emma, still living at home with Uncles Albert and Bobby. I retained some money for myself as between paydays camp administrators used to give us chits or tickets to spend at the cantina to buy personal items, candy, pop, or sundries. They did not sell liquor of any kind. Of course, on payday they took out for the spent chits what we owed so that left us with only five dollars or less. At that time a person could buy a lot with five bucks. When we had passes to go to town, camp staff took us in army trucks and we were expected to be at the pick-up station at a certain time or your ass was mud. If you missed the return ride, you were expected to get back to camp any way that you could.

Promotional ad for the Civilian Conservation Corps. There are a wide variety of these posters in the public domain; I thought this one represented the best scope of work undertaken throughout the country.

Early 1930s photo of Buckeye, Arizona. Courtesy Civilian Conservation Corps, State of Arizona.

The Civilian Conservation Corps

A typical southern Arizona CCC camp constructed in the desert hills; this is one of several camps outside of the Tucson area. Needless to say I am quite sure it was uncomfortably hot during the summers. Courtesy Civilian Conservation Corps, State of Arizona.

Historical photo from Arizona CCC camp work crew building fences. Courtesy Civilian Conservation Corps, State of Arizona.

CHAPTER NINE

Life in the CCC camps came with all sorts of diversions, but in many ways things that happened then were not so different from today as to how life goes on elsewhere. As I had mentioned, not all folks in the CCC were seventeen to twenty years old. Some of the guys were well experienced in life and how to provide themselves spending money. When we went to some towns on liberty, or R&R, some of the older men used to go to town to do what they called "roll the queers." That meant taking the money from these individuals by strong-arming them and getting their cash. Such was the mentality of some men at that time. We inexperienced kids just went to look at the girls, drink a few beers, and do some mischief, though nothing serious, just a little dancing.

The serious stuff with girls was done at camp on payday. The pimps from Phoenix would load their touring sedans with girls of ill repute, ladies of the night, sporting girls, or just plain prostitutes. One could see the vehicles coming through the sand dunes and sagebrush, winding around through the dirt roads, their headlights shining in the night. Two, maybe three cars in a small entourage to make a few dollars off of the CCC personnel. The lines would be formed and waiting, and at night you could tell where the lines were by spotting the lighted cigarettes looking like lightning bugs. Among the sand dunes and sagebrush you could hear the laughing and joking of the guys waiting to get their fifty or seventy-five cents worth of pleasure. While waiting for things to start happening, somebody would bring some beer or a bottle of cheap whiskey and we'd wait with anticipation. Upon arrival the girls would all be dolled up and scatter about the area with their blankets and pillows to get down to business.

Unbelievable, it almost sounds crude, but there was money to be made and willing sellers and willing buyers. The pimps, of course, pocketed most of the money but such was their vocation in life, at least while the girls sold their wares. The following day in the back of the truck we would discuss our good times from the night before; I had some good laughs. In those days the sexual diseases were curable with penicillin; fortunately, it seems the buyers always lucked out and caught nothing.

Because there was so much work to do, the CCC built satellite or side camps in addition to the main headquarters. The camp in Buckeye had a side camp in Fredonia, Arizona, which probably had forty to fifty men stationed there, but when they needed help, they relied on personnel coming over from Buckeye. After being at Buckeye six to eight months, a camp administrator asked for volunteers to go to the Fredonia location (per Dad's records, CCC camp G-170-A, Co. 847). Everything there was the same as the main camp, including meals, work, and discipline, so my friends and I decided we would like a change of scenery and volunteered to go to the side camp.

The trip there by truck must have been a few hundred miles. It was a long ride, but it was something different to experience even though the work was the same. Everything was always first class, at least by my standards. The location that was to be our liberty town was in Kanab, Utah, a small Mormon community. This town was very clean, nice, and friendly. There were some places to hang out but not too many taverns or wild places. It was a typical, quiet, small town, middle America, I suppose, mostly Anglo-Saxon, nice Mormon folks. Good times could be had there as there were not too many CCC personnel to spoil the atmosphere. There were only about fifty to sixty people at the side camp and everybody did not go to town at one time as a group.

My friends and I always hung around together. I don't know why, we just did. We spoke Spanish, of course, when we were together, otherwise we were respectful of the fact that to speak Spanish was not polite. When we went to town, one always could find a good time dancing. There didn't seem to be prejudices about ethnic groups as there were not that many such groups. I never saw any blacks there for whatever reason. We could always buy beer and there was liquor to be bought too. My friends and I didn't have much money, so to make a drink that would give a buzz, we'd purchase a large bottle of beer and a pint of what was called sloe gin, mixing it with the beer. Boy, did this taste good. It went down easy, but wow it could make a person sick, maybe even too sick to die. When we went to dances, there were always girls there looking to have a little fun, dance, have a Coke with a few laughs. My friends and I were all very well behaved. In those times in small towns young people just had a good time. Getting laid was not the ultimate reason to be there at the dances. Those were more simple times, everybody was poor, and trying to impress anybody with anything was not the goal. A lot of the people that we met had relatives in some kind of government program.

I guess I can't say this too often. Life is discipline. If you don't have self-discipline and can't stand to be disciplined, you can have large problems all through life. Being in the CCC taught me that important fact of life. I was in the camps for seventeen months. I've reconsidered the time frame in which I was a part of the CCC camps and as close as I can remember, I joined in March or April 1939. Seventeen months later would be the end of September 1940. I was just a little over eighteen years of age because about six months after I was discharged from the CCC I joined the army. In the time that I was in the CCC, I went home to Tucson maybe three times—the first being just after joining when my grandmother died , and the other two times just to visit.

One particular time that is most clear in my thoughts is when my friends and I all decided to go home together. Except this time was special because we were going to catch a freight train and we thought it would be a blast. We had always hitchhiked before but we thought, "What the heck, let's get going and catch a train, a freight train." It was exciting because we did not really know what to expect. All of us thought it could be dangerous and besides you had to hide from the police at all stops because riding the freight trains was not legal. The authorities would not put a person in jail for doing it, but they took you off the train.

I don't believe that any one of us had done the train bit before, so we talked to other older guys about our plans, some of whom had done it before. After all, we could be macho and afterward brag to our friends at home that we had caught a freight to get there. Somehow, in our talking about catching the freights, one of us found out that somewhere between Phoenix and Fredonia there was a tunnel, and if you were going to catch a train, you had better be in some kind of cover because of the smoke in the tunnel.

When the time came to go home, we caught the freight in

Fredonia and we were on our way. It wasn't too scary, but it was hectic because you had to run close to the train and then jump on to the ladder that all trains have to help the brakeman get on board while on the move. There was a caboose on the train, like they all seemed to have, but we steered clear of it because that is where the brakeman rode. However, we didn't see any of them because it was an empty freight train. I don't remember whether we were carrying anything; we must have had a small bag of clothes. I am sure we were not empty-handed. Riding on top of the train was sort of nice. It was windy and a bit cold. We talked about the tunnel and where it might be, as we had no idea. So we started looking around for a shelter to get out of the smoke in the tunnel when it came. It was not very easy walking on top of freight cars with the train moving, so we moved carefully while trying to maintain our balance.

Finally we found a produce freight car that had the cooler doors open. At one end there were two small lift-up doors where ice was loaded to keep the produce cold while being transported. It was not a small area, as it took up one end of the freight car. The doors were up and we could get into the car. After we entered, we lowered the two doors, enclosing us, but it was too dark, so we opened them up again in order to see while we were getting settled. The tunnel did eventually appear. It wasn't a very long one, but had we been on top of the train, we most certainly would have gotten a hell of a choking from smoke. In all of our concern about being in some sort of shelter before the tunnel came, we failed to notice that this particular freight car had transported garlic, and we now smelled terrible. So we got out and found another empty car that upon our inspection was OK, and it kept us out of the wind, cool air, and garlic smell.

The Civilian Conservation Corps

The train stopped at most little switching stations either to get water or to pick up empty freight cars. In those days they really did not want bums riding the trains, so once in a while a switchman would check for free riders. If you were seen, they would ask you to get off. At one particular stop the yard watchman did find us and asked us where we were going. We said to Tucson because that was where we lived. He asked if we were in the CCC and we told him yes. He told us to stay on and that it was a long way yet to go. That was OK by us. He said, "You guys smell like you rode the empty garlic car. Of all the empty cars you picked that one!" He wished us well and left us thankful that we didn't have to get off the train. After several more hours we arrived at Tucson, home at last. It wasn't a very pleasant trip but it was free and an adventure.

All of my family were happy to see me. Both grandparents had passed away, but there were still several people at the house, including Aunt Emma and Uncles Bobby and Albert. The rest of the family had already started their own homes. Aunt Emma told me how much she appreciated the money I sent home monthly. By all standards we were poor, though not as poor as a lot of other folks. All of the family contributed money to the budget; Emma was a supervisor at Sears, Albert was a sheet metal worker, Bobby worked at a service station, Aunt Molly's husband, Ray, worked for the railroad, and my uncle Tony was a shop foreman at the sheet metal business. Everybody had a job, as the work ethic of the family was that if you work you eat. And the family always had enough money to eat and have a roof over our heads, and family members all drove inexpensive old cars.

My leaves from the CCC camp were fun, I guess, maybe because when they were over, I had the camp to go back to and make a few bucks. After being in Tucson visiting family and friends, then returning to camp, my friends and I realized how lucky we were to be in the CCC. We could see that all the other guys our age were still struggling to make a buck or two.

I believe we took the regular train back to camp, as it wasn't that expensive and it was a lot less dangerous and warmer too than hopping a freight. By this time I had been in the CCC about twelve months, sort of an old-timer. This would be spring of 1940. I would get to come home one more time before my enlistment was up. That would turn out to also be a family visit leave. At the time we still lived at 1250 South 6th Avenue next to Santa Cruz Catholic Church. My time in the CCC was coming to an end. Life in the camps was very much the way I've described to you. All of that time I spent there, I was getting older, a little more mature, becoming a man. I was eighteen in August of 1940. I was discharged from the CCC in late September 1940. Now I had to go home to stay and make a life for myself.

My father's personal photo taken on R&R to Kanab, Utah, with Roberto Ballesteros, a fellow CCC enlistee. Note the Kanab High School in the background. Richard was eighteen in this photograph.

CHAPTER TEN

I was home now. Boy, what a big transition from having someone telling you what to do and when to do it, to where I was now, responsible for all my actions. My first obligation to family and myself was to get a job. I had a little money from the CCC, as they gave me $150 upon discharge, which was severance pay plus a ticket home. The CCC allowed us to keep all of our clothes, which was of some help as they made good work garments. I figured that I would take a few days just to get the idea that work was priority number one. A few more people were working now because the worst of the Depression had passed and things were stirring around. But a person still had to hustle to find work because employers were more interested in experience, and if you were raising a family, those people looking for work received the first opportunity at employment. I wasn't able to get a job right away, but everybody at home knew I was trying, so they encouraged me.

After some time, in October I got a job working for a furniture store, Tucson Furniture Co. as I recall, assisting the truck driver in delivering furniture that was purchased. When I wasn't helping him, I helped the upholsterer to move the furniture he was working on. I always kept busy. It was all routine work doing pretty much the same thing from one day to the next. I didn't get much pay, maybe two dollars a day. I am sure that it couldn't have been more than that because I remember the driver was making five dollars a day and he had been with the company for some time. My job was a fun one because we delivered a lot of happiness: new couches, chairs, mattresses. People were always happy to get these things. I learned about what people expect from you and that everybody appreciates good service. I did a good job, worked hard, and didn't bitch, and my bosses appreciated it. And I now had a little money to be able to help the household. It felt good to be contributing, pulling my own weight.

With my budget I always had a little money left over to get together with my friends to have a good time and treat the girls to a hamburger or a Coke. One of my buddies had an old Model T and it didn't take much gas to make it run. It was also good enough to travel to the mountains with the girls and play a little bit and to try to get into a little mischief. I am sure that then I appreciated female companionship more than before I went into the CCC. We were now into December as the holidays were here and there was a lot of work at the Furniture Co. There were long hours and a little more pay as the job became more routine. I was in good shape, so hard work did not bother me. Into the holiday we had Christmas presents to deliver, and after each delivery we would have cookies, chocolates, and apple cider. Those were really fun times.

On Christmas Eve, after having been delivering furniture, the truck driver decided we needed to get into the Christmas spirit, so he purchased a pint of liquor. Both of us were through working, so we had a couple of good stiff shots, which really felt good after all the hard work. Because I lived a ways from work, the delivery driver gave me a ride home. By this time I was feeling a little woozy. At home on Christmas Eve the family always gathered to celebrate, eat, drink, and have a good time and do family things. At midnight they all went to church, which was just next door. After midnight mass they would come home and continue with the party. It was during the time that people were at midnight mass that I came home; someone was home but no one saw me. I had a room at the back of the house, so I snuck in and went to bed. I was pretty well looped, and when I lay down, the room started to go around and around and I got sick, really sick. I am sure I was too sick to die. And a young man's life continues to unfold . . .

Front page copy of my father's Civilian Conservation Corps discharge papers. I had never seen these until my dad's wife, Joan, gave them to me along with his army papers after my father passed.

Two for You, One for Me

```
              RECORD OF SERVICE IN CIVILIAN CONSERVATION CORPS

**Served:                                            Camp G-109-A
a. From 4-18-39  to  4-15-40  under Interior  Dept. at Arlington, Arizona
   Type of work Fence Construction  *Manner of performance Satisfactory
                                                     Camp G-138-A
b. From 4-16-40  to  8-10-40  under War       Dept. at Short Creek, Ariz.
   Type of work Camp Construction  *Manner of performance Satisfactory
                                                     Camp G-170-A
c. From 8-10-40  to  9-30-40  under Interior  Dept. at Fredonia, Arizona
   Type of work Fence Construction  *Manner of performance Satisfactory
d. From _____ to _____ under _____ Dept. at _____
   Type of work _____ *Manner of performance _____
e. From _____ to _____ under _____ Dept. at _____
   Type of work _____ *Manner of performance _____

   Future Address of enrollee:
Last Discharged from Co. 847, CCC, Camp G-170-A, Fredonia, Arizona
Enrollee has been notified that he cannot be again accepted for
enrollment for a period of six months from date of discharge
Education: 7th Grade                  Occupation: Laborer
Enrollee's Serial Number: CC8-8471227
Company Commander's Estimate of Individual Satisfactory
Fingerprint card submitted: April 28, 1939
Final pay roll furnished to include date of discharge
Paid in Full $ 14.75              F. W. MOORE, Major (Inf) F. D.,
By _____  JOHN L. ERICKSON, Company Commander CCC
Special Agent

                                       Camp G-170-A Co. 847
Discharged: Honorably, Sept. 30, 1940 at Fredonia, Arizona
Transportation furnished from Cedar City, Utah to Tucson, Arizona

                    JOHN L. ERICKSON, Company Commander
                               (Name)                (Title)
*Use words "Excellent", "Satisfactory", or "Unsatisfactory". Commanding
**To be taken from U. C. C. Form No. L.
Arizona Junior
```

Back page of CCC discharge document details my father's service work record, physical locations of camp numbers, and location names. Sorry for the discoloration of the top quarter of a document that had been folded for many, many years.

PART FOUR

OCTOBER 1940– NOVEMBER 1941

An Army Life Takes Me Further from My Roots and Culture;
Speaking English Is an Army Requirement

The Three Amigos, 1941, Fort Bliss, Texas. Frank Hughes, Richard Hernández, and Ernesto Acuña. Photo from my father's service album and his personal, metal coat of arms insignia of purple and gold colors.

COAT OF ARMS
63RD COAST ARTILLERY ANTIAIRCRAFT

AMOR PATRIAE (LOVE OF COUNTRY)

CHAPTER ELEVEN

With continued improvement in the making of a new life, an environment of better things to come, I grew further and further from a previous life that to this day is still fresh in my mind in many ways. Joining the army was just another step in my growing up and becoming part of a larger world experience. It was very similar to my experience when I joined the CCC, but on a much grander scale. I was eighteen and a half years old at the time. Ernest Acuña, Frank Hughes, and I were still palling around together, and in January of 1941 we decided that we had enjoyed our time spent in the CCC camps, so we asked ourselves: Should the navy be our next step? At that time the Depression was slowly winding down and economic activity was beginning to stir and things seemed to be improving. When you are eighteen years old, times are restless and schooling doesn't seem too exciting. I guess that, for me, school was the least important, and both the navy and the army had a drive to increase the armed forces. The three of us were inclined to choose the navy, though neither one of us knew much about ships or oceans, but one could travel and see things and this sounded exciting to all of us. And besides, navy uniforms looked so neat and striking, and we'd get to see the world.

The three of us made an appointment with the navy recruiter and also stopped by and made one with the army as well. Now we only had to choose which branch of the service we would join. The night we were supposed to decide, we all got drunk and, of course, the next day we missed our navy appointment. So we headed for the army office, whose recruiter was happy to see us, so we joined. Since we had just six months prior been discharged from the CCC camps, we felt certain we had some idea of what army life would be like and were ready for a new adventure. After being sworn in, examined, and found to be healthy and full of energy, we three amigos were accepted. We settled all the paperwork with the recruiter and were told to report in the morning to the recruiting office in order to be sent to the army post where we were assigned. I have often wondered how different my life would have been had my friends and I not missed the navy appointment. Funny how an incident such as that perhaps totally changed the course of how my life was yet to unfold.

The next morning we three amigos showed up at the army recruiting office with sunshiny faces. We were joined by many other men, some of whom were volunteers and others draftees. All of us were sent to Fort Bliss located in El Paso, Texas. All were trucked to the Tucson train depot where we were met by army personnel and then directed to board the train bound for Texas. At the train station there were recruiting posters plastered all over the walls with Uncle Sam telling us he wanted us. He was pointing at me and here I was!

Fort Bliss was a cavalry unit. In the past wars you would associate such a unit with horses, typically for mobilization of personnel and war materiel, as well as attacking the enemy. While they did in fact have horses, this post was a mechanized cavalry unit.

An Army Life Takes Me Further from My Roots

Upon our arrival at the fort, we were trucked to our assigned post, the 63rd Coast Artillery Batteries. This was an antiaircraft unit that was sited up on a hillside together with the 200th and 202nd Coast Artillery Batteries. From the bottom of this hillside where the main highway was located, you could see rows and rows of tents. These had been put up to receive all the new recruits who were training to become soldiers. These camps were manned by regular army soldiers, older men, most of them seasoned soldiers and mean as sin. Many of these individuals had served in China, the Philippines, or Hawaii and they were all noncommissioned officers. These men demanded and got respect. We learned from our instructors that when these non-coms gave orders, we recruits responded and acted accordingly.

As our group was greeted by our non-coms in charge, each of us was assigned to quarters, tents in this case, with wooden floors and neatly arranged bunks with mattresses. We were informed that our company was B Battery of the 63rd Coast Artillery, and then ordered to go to the supply room where each person got outfitted with their gear, including uniforms and other clothing, footlockers, rifles, ammunition belts—just about everything one would ever need. Our battery first sergeant was Sergeant Arbelo, a Cuban with twenty to twenty-five years of service. He had a very low, harsh, gruff voice and all the authority to do anything. My buddies and I understood authority, having experienced it for eighteen months in the CCC camps. But this type of authority was a few notches more authoritative and more serious! Our tent assignments were given to us by our assigned non-com. I don't believe we had a choice which tent we wanted.

My particular tent assignment was interesting. We were all enlistees. I was the youngest while five other guys were twenty-five years old, and the real old man was thirty-six; we had men from New York, New Jersey, Indiana, and Arizona. Our ethnic origins included Polish, Irish, Italian, Jewish, and one Hispanic, me. These were men with families and jobs and good upbringing as well as education—good men all of them. They were all mature and well stationed in their respective communities: electricians, policemen, carpenters, truck drivers, well-rounded, responsible people. How different I was from these other older guys; I was still wet behind the ears. I felt proud to be with such high-caliber men. These fellows reflected all that this country used to be proud of, full of confidence, strength, hardworking men with integrity. We were all focused, desiring to do the same thing, serving our country.

At the time Arizona to me seemed such a small state, while these men from other cultural backgrounds and characteristics seemed to be altogether different from my experience. In Tucson the cultural structure was mostly Hispanic, with some Caucasians and fewer African Americans. My Fort Bliss tent included Breen (Irish), Novotny (Polish), Bruno (Italian), Altman (Jewish), Schwartz (German), and me. I grew to love all of these guys and most of all love the army. The men all got along just fine and teased the hell out of each other.

Training exercises in the days and weeks ahead became our lives' focus in order to become soldiers. There never was too much time to play. For six to eight weeks all we did was train to become good at taking orders, cleaning camp, and doing duties to maintain a good, disciplined attitude. Learning to take orders when they were given to you and to take and implement them without question was drilled into us. Most of all we had to learn about guns: rifles, machine guns, automatic rifles, and Tommy Guns, including our big three-inch antiaircraft guns. Day in and day out we would be exhausted by nighttime from all the studying, learning, watching movies about why we were learning to fight and who we were going to fight, and bayonet and firing range training. At that time the only arms we had to train with were old 1903 Springfield rifles. We would take them apart and put them back together in light, dark, and blindfolded conditions. Occasionally we were assigned KP (kitchen police), which meant peeling potatoes, doing dishes, mopping floors, washing pans. Whatever needed doing in the kitchen we did. All in all we were functioning like a well-oiled machine, keeping ourselves well polished and sharp looking while getting to know each other very well.

Building friendships was an indirect result of the intense training we were all undertaking. Frank Hughes, Ernie Acuña, and I were good friends, but we each were building other friendships and learning how other people from other parts of the country lived and how they celebrated their festivities. From us the others learned how things were in the southwest, and being close to El Paso and Juarez, we all were to learn a lot more.

Army life was never boring even though we didn't have passes to go to town. We did other fun things such as played baseball and pool, and used the rec rooms, which sold sundries except liquor or beer—that was to come later, as someone would always secure a bottle and life would go on. The men worked hard and whatever pleasure one could get was well deserved. As a group we all got along fine; there were very few men who caused trouble, mainly because it was not tolerated. Army life kept everyone busy enough so that there were better things to do than to look for or cause trouble. Sometimes when we were allowed to rest and enjoy some time off, I would think about how lucky I was to have been in the CCC prior to the army. It was in that setting that I was taught a lot about discipline, cleanliness, how to take care of personal things, to have self-respect, to respect authority, and just how to be a good citizen. What I learned both in the CCC and the army, to a large measure, made me the person that I am today.

In the early army days money was always in need as income was only twenty-one dollars per month for enlistees. One means to increase one's personal cash was to participate in card games that seemed to start up at a moment's notice. Most of the soldiers in my battery were men with a lot of experience in life, so many of them gambled. Somebody always won while someone always lost. Plus there were always some card sharks around, mainly the old non-coms, sergeants, corporals, and old soldiers that had made the army their lives. It seemed that they always had money to lend people who wanted it at some ridiculously high interest rate, seven to ten dollars for thirteen dollars paid back. On payday these loan sharks always waited at the end of the pay line to settle and collect their debts, and you paid! I never borrowed money because I couldn't afford to pay their prices.

One particular shark, an old-time soldier staff sergeant, a career type, owned a beautiful red Buick convertible, which was frequently occupied by a gorgeous blonde in the front seat. She would come after hours and wait for the sergeant. On paydays he would collect the most money, even having a little table he would set up for processing his debtors. He couldn't lose; he sat at the end of the pay table and those who owed him money paid him in cash while he sat there sucking on his big cigar, stacking his money on his little table, counting your change if you had any coming back. But everybody who needed money after payday wanted to know him personally.

Finally our training weeks came to an end and we were all

excited about going to El Paso for some rest and relaxation, R&R. And if you had some balls, you'd go to Juarez. That could be a little testy because the Mexican guys did not appreciate American soldiers coming across the border to solicit their women, even with what little money the soldiers had in their pockets. All of us were made aware that only in civilian clothes could you go to Mexico, so if you were in uniform, you had to stay in El Paso.

The first time I went to El Paso, I was with Ernie and Frank, my buddies, so we thought we had a little advantage because we could speak the language and had a little money. So we piled in a truck along with other soldiers and were taken to a set place and dumped off, with the truck to return at a certain time. If you were there when the truck came back, you got a ride, and if you were not, you had to make your own way back to camp, either hoof it, taxi, or hitchhike. All of us had a good time eating Mexican food, had a few drinks, and watched other soldiers get into trouble after they had a few too many. Since Ernie, Frank, and I were in uniform, we stayed in El Paso; even so, there were many opportunities to get into trouble. Of course there were Military Police (MPs) all over the place, which was reassuring because they brought a sense of security to the area.

When you first went to town on leave, normally one would find a place that was crowded with others of your own kind, the more soldiers the better. When you visited again, then you found your own good times. In those days it was not uncommon to frequent the cantinas that were also places of ill repute, offering the men an opportunity for a good time. However, you had to be careful not to be too accommodating to the women because there were the regular Mexican clientele and they wanted their share of female companionship, so one had to be cool. The primary thing to keep in mind while on leave was that it was most important above all to be in camp by battery inspection. I was always in camp when I had to be.

Our camp, comprised of the 63rd, 200th, and 202nd Coast Artilleries, occupied an area made up of an entire hillside at Fort Bliss. It was quite a site, neat, orderly, and made up of men who were all becoming what we were supposed to be: good soldiers. I suppose all the army personnel came to about 3,500 to 4,000 men, each unit always trying and striving to be the unit that was the most outstanding. There were parades and lots of inspections by high-ranking army generals. There was a continuous building up of draftees and enlistees from all over the country to increase the strength of the armed forces. At the same time the camp was receiving newer and more technical equipment. Days all became the same, though with increasingly different people from dissimilar cultures, very unlike from when we first reported to camp.

When the men had a little bit of time for R&R, the trips to El Paso became the thing to look forward to. And since those who had been here longer thought we knew the ropes, the new guys could learn a thing or two from us as we were getting to know our way around the fun spots and where the pretty women were located. The first time I had the pleasure of a woman was at one of these cantinas catering to soldiers. The ladies there were pretty and after a couple of drinks they got even prettier and would accommodate any fantasies a man could muster. For fifty cents you could have a good time.

On my first sexual encounter I took this lovely woman to her room and I was feeling like I could hold my own with this experienced lady. We got undressed and into bed and proceeded to make love. I must say I didn't last long and it was all over. It was quite an experience and she asked me if I was finished. She knew damn well I was, so I answered "yes" and then she told me to get off of her as I was costing her money and she had to work for a living. She asked me to be sure and come back to see her again when I was in town. It took me longer to get dressed than it did to make love, but such is life for a young soldier. Now that I am older, it seems such a memory about that first time; it's almost funny but such memories last a long while. And so life goes on and as you get older, those are the things that you sometimes think about in passing. Some memories are sad, some are better, some are out of this world, and some you would do differently but you only get one chance.

CHAPTER TWELVE

The army life always seemed to offer the same things with some variations. As time went by, some changes were taking place and one day Sergeant Carlson asked Ernie, Frank, and me to report to Sergeant Arbelo. That could mean almost anything, good or bad news. Sergeant Arbelo, as I mentioned earlier, was a Cuban and a man of authority and well disciplined. We reported to him and he told us to be at ease. All three of us listened carefully while the sergeant told us how well we were doing and that there had been good reports from all of our non-coms. By now we had been in the service for perhaps four to five months. The sergeant then told us we were going to have to change something that we were doing but that it was going to benefit us during our army stay, and as we become noncommissioned officers when we're ready. He informed us that he spoke Spanish and that he loved to speak his language and he knew that we did as well. He then told us that each of us must begin to speak English even when just we three were together, as it would improve our relationships with our English-speaking friends, and we would benefit by learning more of the language than we currently knew. He then told us that when we enlisted in the army we made a good and smart decision and we would improve our opportunities for promotion by following his advice. Sergeant Arbelo ended the conversation by telling us not to forget what we had talked about and that he would inform a pleased battery commander that we had this discussion; we were then excused.

As I mentioned earlier, the army was in an expansion mode and they were vigorously evaluating existing personnel to determine their strengths and weaknesses, and how well men could do certain things, both mentally and physically. Were you a slow or fast learner? How well could you react to certain situations? Could you be taught easily? How intelligent were you? Everybody was required to take the army aptitude tests, which included about 150 questions designed to probe all kinds of areas. The army felt these tests would provide them with valuable information about personnel, which could then be used in deciding the most effective and appropriate roles for each individual soldier. Once these tests were completed, it was back to army training and some different challenges. All this time the men continued to be evaluated by their superiors, who were deciding what each person could do best to contribute to the collective effort, keeping in mind that a functioning artillery battery is composed of a multitude of different duties such as truck drivers, gun crews, radar technicians, searchlight operators, and office personnel.

Finally the time came for each of us to be assigned to whatever an individual could do best to help the overall effort. Sergeant Arbelo assembled the battery personnel and we all stood at attention and waited to be addressed by the battery commander. He made us stand at ease and proceeded to explain that we had accomplished during the past several months all that was required at this stage and that our basic training was now officially over. It was now time to proceed on to other things, more of the same except more focused as we would now report to specific units to which each would be assigned. Sergeant Arbelo then told us that we had done very well in our learning of army ways and that he expected us to become the best battery in the 63rd Coast Artillery. He then turned the battery over to the sergeants and corporals to do their thing. They explained to us that each of us would be asked what types of jobs each wanted to do while in the army.

We then broke into smaller groups with a sergeant that asked each soldier what job interested them, and each person was then assigned to that particular role. Some guys wanted to be in gun crews, radar, truck drivers, mechanics, searchlights, and such, all real nice assignments, of course. I wanted to be a truck driver because I didn't know how to drive anyway so I thought it would be a good place to learn. All the men then gathered together according to training group preferences. Then out of the goodness of their hearts, the sergeants said that if anybody wanted to change their job category, this would be a good time to do so. After we were all satisfied that we had made a good choice, the sergeant assigned some corporals to take over the detail and to present us to our job choices.

My group was called to attention by the corporal and another corporal watched. We were then told that we were going to march to the motor pool, and when we arrived there, I was astonished at all of the big equipment, including backhoes, bulldozers, dump trucks, and all kinds of other vehicles, mostly all new. Some of the really big trucks were prime movers that hauled the three-inch guns because these guns were quite heavy. The corporal then surprised us all when he told us that some of us would probably end up driving these babies. I thought this was going to be really something! The corporal then proceeded to compliment us on our choice of assignment and told us who was in charge of the motor pool and how many trucks we had. He then called us to attention and pointed to a huge stock of wheelbarrows and told us to select one and report back in line. We all laughed and were thinking, "Sure we're going to be truck drivers, and will be the first to drive these lovely wheelbarrows," then returned to our places in line. Wheelbarrows and all, we were then marched to a huge pile of dirt, rocks, and sagebrush.

Our particular camp and area was constructed on a hillside full of rocks, and in order to make room for all of the tents, the earth had been bulldozed into a huge pile. The army was making room to receive all of the new men and we were the new men. We were told that the pile had to be moved and that the moving equipment could not get to the pile due to all of the new tents having been put up. We were the truck drivers who would move the dirt while also operating the shovels to fill the wheelbarrows. It was quite funny after we thought about it, and, of course, we all laughed about how everybody had put this little joke over on the new guys. It was OK though; it was fun. I believe that the other job categories had similar experiences. They worked us very hard, which made us all really hungry. Later in the day in the mess hall, all of us laughed at our jobs. We were done with this huge task in about a week's time though it was hard work with the sun beating down on us. The moving of this mountain also reinforced discipline and doing what you are told to do and don't ask questions. At the same time it toughened us up and taught us that as a group, and individually, we could take whatever was dished out.

There were always tasks to do and everything that we did taught us something. All of us were becoming more aware of what was expected of us as soldiers, so that for everything demanded of me I did to the very best of my ability and I was always willing to learn more. I loved the army and all that went with it. Frank, Ernie, and I stilled palled together and we had made the transition from speaking in Spanish to using only English. And although it sounded funny to us, we still spoke it and thereafter nobody could question what our conversations were about. As a result of our using exclusively the English language, our vocabularies expanded and our abilities to converse improved, though we retained our native accents somewhat, which was OK.

One day Sergeant Arbelo called me into his office, and when I reported to him, he said to me "Private Hernández, the battery commander has asked me to talk to you about your aptitude test results." I imagined I probably didn't do very well since I had no formal education and very little practical knowledge other than the CCC. So he continued, saying, "As you know, the army is increasing the armed forces and there is a severe shortage of officers that can assume responsibilities. The army is looking for men that have shown a good ability during their basic training and who have stayed out of trouble during the time they have been in the service. These considerations contribute to making a person's potential. All of these factors fit you just right. Your aptitude test was well above average and the commander would like you to consider the opportunity of becoming an officer. Will you think about our little talk and let me know how you feel about making such a move?Whatever you decide, you should know that the army will send you to school and teach you all that you have to know. Private Hernández, you are excused."

First, I must say that I was scared at such an opportunity, though I told the Sergeant that I would think about it. I went back to my tent and I thought to myself, "Doesn't the army know that my education is way below par and I couldn't do anything about it at that time?" In addition, my English and ability to communicate was still poor. Then I thought about our two second lieutenants that we had in Battery B. They were young and inexperienced and new at their jobs as officers. Of course the men made fun of them behind their backs because they were still learning. However, the young officers always had our respect and we obeyed their commands. The old corporals and sergeants were all very knowledgeable and tough and they backed the younger officers while they were learning.

While there was still a lot of learning to do and training to be done, I thought about what Sergeant Arbelo had said to me concerning the officer training school opportunity. When such a promotion is offered to you, one must get realistic about all that is expected of oneself, and all of the responsibility put on you to do the right thing. At that time in my life I just could not imagine how a person with no formal education could learn all the critical schooling and then be able to direct other men and expect them to do what you told them to do. A lot of the draftees coming into the service at that time were educated, mature family folks who were used to taking orders from and giving them to other mature individuals. On the other hand, I saw myself as just an uneducated kid from the other side of the tracks. And even though a growing army with young officers was in the making and doing quite well at it, I felt that I could not do the job as an officer, but I could be a good, honest, hardworking, and proud enlisted man. With my lack of education I feared the unknown, so I chose not to accept the offer of officer training school. The opportunity just died in limbo as I never followed up with Sergeant Arbelo. I sometimes think about what might have been but never was . . .

Army life continued to function and things happened that made it more interesting. Sergeant Arbelo called me into his office one day and said to me, "Private Hernández, can you drive?" I said sure but I really did not know how to drive. When at home I had tried learning on a Model T once or twice. My uncle Bobby had tried to teach me to drive a Model A Ford, but I damned near had an accident so he gave up on me. That was the extent of my driving instructions. The sergeant then told me that starting next week he wanted me to be ready to be on call whenever the battery commander needed to go someplace. The commander usually went to Fort Bliss three times a week for meetings and sometimes traveled to other areas to meet with other battery commanders. Wherever he wished to go, the vehicle and I were to be ready. Sergeant Arbelo then told me that I was to go to the motor pool that week and talk to the sergeant in charge and do whatever I needed to learn all that I could about the captain's car. And another thing, I was to make sure that I was personally ready to go, including having polished shoes and brass buttons as well as a pressed uniform and haircut. I was not to worry about making small talk with the captain, just be his driver.

So I went to the motor pool and spoke to the sergeant and explained why I was there and asked him if he could show me where the captain's car was parked. This particular sergeant was an old-timer and talking to young recruits was not the best thing he did. He asked me if I knew how to drive and I told him yes, a little bit. He responded with "How little?" as he sensed I was not a first-class driver. He informed me that these army vehicles were a lot harder to drive than civilian cars, so he had better show me a thing or two. I said thank you. He indicated to me that he would help me if I felt I needed it, but if not then I could try it first and let him know. I said to him that if he didn't mind he could first show me. He then asked me if I had ever had a driver's license, and I told him no but that I believed that I could pass the driving test if he was to teach me.

The sergeant turned out to be very good to me and told me that a lot of drivers were not really sure about these vehicles and that some time had to be spent teaching most drivers. He got in the driver's seat and I climbed in on the other side. He pointed out the ignition switch and the gearshift and explained that the gearshift was numbered so you knew what gear you were in and how to shift the gears. He also explained the clutch, brake, and gas pedal locations and functions. He then told me that I would do all right and that he was going to teach me as if I didn't know anything, so to take my time and watch what he did. The sergeant told me that the clutch was the tricky part, but once I got the feel, the rest was easy. He demonstrated to me the mechanics of operating the pedals and drove the car over to where other soldiers were getting their instructions. Then it was my turn to drive. He handed me the keys and told me not to be nervous, and that I would do just fine.

I was so nervous my knees were shaking as I looked to see that everything was clear. I put the key into the ignition and put the gearshift into neutral, pushed in the clutch, turned on the ignition, and started the car. I also took a deep breath and then put the car into forward gear and released the clutch and then all hell broke loose. The vehicle began a bucking bronco routine and the sergeant quickly told me to depress the clutch and to try once again, only releasing the clutch more easily. So I attempted this several times and somehow it got better as I began to get the feel of releasing the clutch. The sergeant then suggested we talk a little about my driving experience and the types of cars I had driven. I recounted my driving Ford Model As and Ts. He listened and then told me that I really needed to get busy with learning as fast as I could since I had only five days to be prepared to drive, as I had been temporarily assigned to the motor pool. He told me that he would help me learn and that he would talk to my first sergeant to relieve me from other duties. I could then put all of my time into learning and practicing to drive.

With the help of the motor pool sergeant, I learned all the necessary skills to drive. The only thing I had left to master was the fear of driving in traffic. After a couple of test runs with the motor pool, the sergeant said I was ready. Fort Bliss was about twelve miles from where our camp was located on a hill, the roads were narrow, and to get to the main road elevation, one had to descend down. Since Fort Bliss was a cavalry post, there were lots of horses and other motorized traffic on the roads, and at the post itself, there was lots of traffic. The army was very strict about speed limits so that was my saving grace. Well, now the acid test was about to begin, but I was quite comfortable as I had been practicing around the area and had solved all the clutch and gearshift problems.

On a Monday my new assignment started and over the PA system comes the sergeant's voice: "Private Hernández, please report to the first sergeant's tent." I hastily went and when I arrived, the first sergeant says to me that the battery commander wanted to go to Fort Bliss today and that I should get the commander's car and myself all polished up. I completed all my personal items, including shined shoes, polished brass, and ironed shirt and pants, and when completed, I walked over to the motor pool office to get the keys, which were on a board with a vehicle number. Since the sergeant was not there and the commander's car was parked behind a two-and-a-half-ton truck, and I could not find a soul to get the truck moved, I went back to the keyboard and got the key to the truck. I decided it was now or never. This was totally out of my experience but by some miracle I was able to move the truck just enough to be able to retrieve the commander's car. Whew!

At the time I still had not received my driver's license though the sergeant told me he would provide me with one. But for some reason, the processing had not yet been completed. Anyway, on my first trip to Fort Bliss I did not have an official driver's license. I went to get the commander's car and proceeded to the first sergeant's tent, and while I waited for the battery commander, I dusted the car seats and the dashboard and generally have the vehicle sparkling for the officer. As I polished the car, the first sergeant came out and talked to me about being ready. I indicated I was prepared and waited for my passenger to arrive. While I was waiting, the wind was blowing, and since none of the roads were paved, dust continued to settle on Private Hernández's command car. Finally I saw the battery commander coming up the street, and it wouldn't be long now before I must put my driving skills to the test. As the officer came over, I saluted him and he said he would be just a minute in the first sergeant's tent and was soon back. He climbed into the car and said he wanted to go to Fort Bliss and that he would direct me to the destination of his meeting when we arrived at the fort. I said, "Yes Sir." I didn't have to worry about carrying on a conversation, so I just concentrated on my driving.

It was about two miles to the main road, two miles of what seemed like a hell of a lot of dust, oncoming trucks up the hill, and truck traffic going down the hill. Nobody was passing because the speed was limited to the road conditions, which were slow. I thought that I was doing just fine because all that I had to do was think of what to do next as my driving at that time was not at all automatic; I had to plan my every move. The twelve miles to Fort Bliss were without incident as the military traffic, though considerable, was congested and slow. Once at the fort, traffic was more complicated because of the horses that were also part of the fort's transportation; consequently, I had to be more careful. Once at the post the battery commander directed me to where I had to go, so it was easier for me. When we arrived at the meeting place, there was lots of room to park, so things turned out just fine. The officer dismounted and we saluted each other, and then my job was to polish the car while I waited and try to look as sharp as I could. I was very proud of myself and to have the job that I was doing.

At this time my basic training had been over for about two months, and I felt like a soldier who was ready for whatever was asked of me. This was still a peacetime army but in very serious training to become the best that there was. Because of my job I could bypass wheelbarrow details and other less important duties. The training was still going on, though army life was very much the same day in and day out: hikes with full packs, rifle training, always learning about weapons, maintaining ourselves in good condition, some recreation, and always more training. My friends and I were still excited about what we were involved in. We were meeting a lot of different people, learning that we think, talk, and react differently to certain situations while always being dependent upon one another to a point. Frank and Ernie and I were the only Hispanic enlistees or draftees in our battery composed of 175 to 200 men. The Spanish language was still our preferred mode of communication amongst ourselves but hardly ever used in close company with others. We made every effort to speak English in our

our dealings with others, and all three of us continued to improve our language skills.

One day Sergeant Arbelo called me into his tent and I reported to him, thinking that he wanted me to get the commander's car ready. Instead, he wanted to talk about something that he and I had discussed some months earlier; he wanted to know what I had decided to do about officer training school. It took me a long time to try to tell him that I really did not feel comfortable proceeding with the opportunity. I told him my lack of education did not help my confidence in undertaking such a responsibility and that I was happy with what I was doing, that I would work really hard to become a noncommissioned officer. He said he understood and just to continue doing the good work that I was. Sergeant Arbelo also indicated the battery commander had approved a change in rank to private first class, and that I certainly deserved it! This promotion increased my pay somewhat but also increased my responsibilities. I was so proud of myself. My friends Frank and Ernie made fun of this captain's driver, but the joke was short-lived as they both received a change in rank a few weeks later. I told them I had put in a good word for both with the captain. But we were all doing a good job and we earned our first stripe.

Sergeant P.A. Arbelo on the left, the other two sergeants are from Battery "B" as well. Photo from my father's album.

CHAPTER THIRTEEN

In June 1941 additional changes came about as more new draftees arrived at Fort Bliss from other parts of the country, including Oklahoma, Louisiana, Missouri, Kentucky, Texas, New Mexico, and other states. Ernie, Frank, and I were still the only Hispanics in B Battery, 63rd Coast Artillery. This influx of personnel from somewhere other than the East Coast created a somewhat newer environment with the mix of different cultures, less educated compared to East Coasters, different work skills and tougher attitudes, but everybody was willing to accept the differences and become a united team. However, some conflicts did occur and differences in ethnic backgrounds did influence some comments. Although made in jest, these comments still were noticeable. Guys from the Deep South and guys from the North would discuss the Civil War as a bad part of history. By and large we all were men and getting ready to do a job that we thought might need to be done. The Japanese were in some intense diplomatic discussions with the United States, something about oil and steel junk that they used to buy from this country that Japan still needed but was no longer getting from us.

Our training as always was still ongoing, the hikes became

more frequent, the training films became more intense, and then the rumor started about Louisiana Maneuvers. This was supposed to be the heavier training, as close to combat as possible, and possibly at the time the largest war training exercise ever undertaken in our country by the armed services. Our activity became more and more rough and increasingly demanding. Our morale became higher as we battled through the obstacle course that now included live ammunition, jumping barricades, and crawling through the mud under barbed wire, coupled with long drives in the trucks that seemed to last forever at thirty-five miles per hour, making for long days and nights. As an army we were really getting ready for Louisiana war training. I was still driving the captain's car, but there was something about the gun crews that seemed more like what I'd prefer to be doing. My friends were there doing all of the exciting stuff and I wanted to be part of that activity. I requested a transfer and became part of a gun crew under Sergeant W.W. Cooper, a really nice guy. We became close friends and remained so after the war.

Come September soldiers and materiel in training camps throughout the country were scheduled to go to Louisiana and undertake war games, referred to as the Louisiana Maneuvers, the largest military war exercise ever conducted by this country at that time, maybe even to today. We comprised two armies in size once we were all gathered in Louisiana. The Second and Third Armies were to "battle" one another, having I believe a total number of troops of close to a half-million men. That was one hell of a lot of soldiers and materiel concentrated in one geographical area. Our departure from El Paso became a long, serpentine convoy made up of the 200th, 202nd, and 63rd Coast Artilleries; what a fantastic sight to observe such a number of men and materiel. With all of our equipment we covered many miles of highway with a lot of great experiences and very exciting situations that made everybody very proud and helped to build morale. Our convoy went through several towns and a lot of beautiful country that many of us had never seen before, including miles and miles of white sands in New Mexico. Our convoys stopped at these sand dunes and the men played around in them as they were most interesting, then off we would go again at thirty-five miles per hour.

You can imagine that we did not cover a lot of territory. We drove through New Mexico, though I don't remember whether we drove day and night. I do remember that we made four real stops to bivouac overnight. I believe we stopped at Pecos, Abilene, Dallas, and White Lake, all in Texas.

I had never before seen such big bodies of water, so I thought White Lake, located outside of Dallas, was large. At that time in 1941 there was very little there, just side roads, a few houses scattered about, and mostly poor neighborhoods. Since Dallas was located seven hundred miles from El Paso, we had to unload all our equipment and check everything out, so we stayed there two nights. All of us very much appreciated the layover and the opportunity to hustle a beer or two.

There also were some women who came to see the soldiers. In the army there were different levels of knowledge of how to score with the ladies when there was a chance. I wasn't one of those smart guys. The older men seemed to have all the tricks up their sleeves. At nineteen years old I had some learning to do about how to get close to women. It was a lot of fun for most of us, and I believe most of the experienced men got in to see the main Dallas areas. When we left after two days, there were some good friendships made with some of the local women. But as they say, love 'em and leave 'em. The country at that time had a good feeling about the armed forces, and the people displayed their pride to us soldiers and we all appreciated their kindness. Of course, with all of our men and materiel we looked like we meant business and were really serious about all that we were doing; this was an army on the move.

From Dallas the convoys headed toward Shreveport, Louisiana, and from there traveled to other places as part of the war maneuvers, going to Alexandria, Lake Charles, and around neighboring towns, though we never quite made it to New Orleans. The war games turned out to be most interesting. I've said many times that army life was pretty much the same from day to day, but this experience was no ordinary exercise. This was a war, or damn close to it, with all the realities that made a warlike environment and experience. In a way it was fun, but hard work. Long, long days and nights, not much rest, you'd put up the equipment and then break it down, and then move to another location. The weather in Louisiana was the worst I had ever experienced; with humid, choking heat, a person could not get dry in the stifling conditions. In addition, we had to deal with swamps, snakes, leeches, mosquitoes, insects of all kinds. You name it, Louisiana had it.

While in Louisiana we managed to have some fun times on our liberty passes that didn't come often enough. When passes were handed out, we all seemed to enjoy ourselves as things could get rather wild; after all, we had money and needed some real live action. When it was possible to do so, that meant visiting houses of ill repute to enjoy female company. Since I wasn't comfortable paying for women, and was concerned about venereal disease, I didn't purchase pleasure, but the crazy things that we did in those houses was unbelievable. The guys would get together and there always was a hearty soul who had more nerve than most of us. A lot of the men were married and had kids back home and chose to respect their marriages. They, nonetheless, participated by going along and watching others enjoy themselves. Our group paid the prostitutes to take on some of the most active guys, and there were some that could put on quite a show for us watchers. Now, as I write this, it really sounds like a poor choice, but back then after a few beers and lots of activity conducive to a sexual atmosphere, it was fun to be there. When we were in a house of fun, it was loud and there were lots of prostitutes just hanging on to any and all prospects. I wasn't a prospect but I did enjoy the attention.

On one of our leaves in Alexandria, Louisiana, we were all full of energy and a lot of it was mischievous. We found ourselves in this little town and our goal was to have fun. In our battery there was a guy whose name was Altman. He was a Jewish guy from the Bronx and a hell-raiser. He was about five feet five and he had a manhood that was all of twelve inches relaxed. In the showers we'd all joke about it. This one time several of us asked Altman if he would let us watch if we paid for a prostitute for him. He said sure, so we took him to a sporting house and had a few beers after which the gang decided it was time for Altman to get laid. So we all ponied up some money and collected ten dollars.

Now to find the lady that would consent to having an audience of eight to ten fellows. We found this small gal about five foot two and well-built and asked her if she would have sex with one of us while the others watched. She thought about it and we told her we would pay her ten dollars. Well that was about five tricks for her, so she said sure and told us to follow her as she asked us who the guy was going to be. One of us pointed to Altman and heck, he was such a small man in stature because he had gone all to cock.

She looked him over and said, "OK," and we all followed her to the room where we were sure to see a gigantic show. They proceeded to get undressed; of course, there were all kinds of comments. She got on the bed while Altman took off his shorts. He then jumped into bed with her with his manhood hanging practically to his knees; you can imagine how large he was at the ready. She began to get herself positioned and then she said, "Whoa! Just a minute. I can't take that thing and expect to stay in business, at least not for the rest of the day." She then jumped out of bed and got herself together and told us to keep our money but she did know a lady in the house who could handle him.

We told her to bring her in and then she was gone for a few minutes. A different woman then came in and asked, "Who was the giant here?" We pointed to Altman as we all were laughing. This new lady then said she needed first to get paid ten dollars. They then proceeded to get down to business and there were a few groans and grunts. The rest of us were all laughing and drinking our beers; it was quite a show. She actually screamed, maybe with pleasure, anyway we all thought we had gotten our money's worth. Well, it is fair to say that this particular day was one that was different from all of the rest up until that time, and one that has not been forgotten.

All of these activities were releases for us to help put aside the fact that personnel were many times exposed to very dangerous situations while on these maneuvers. Often one would be exhausted and sleep was something that none of us got much of in the swamps. While we were standing by, you'd grab a quick snooze. There were many serious accidents with trucks driving through the swamps in the darkness and running over sleeping soldiers. There was no way a truck driver could be aware of a

An Army Life Takes Me Further from My Roots

sleeping GI next to a gun position or near a camp area, let alone knowing where one was in relation to any of these guns or camp areas. There were several fatal accidents. Even with all the dangers and bad accidents, the whole maneuver experience was still fantastic and very exciting.

The time from mid-September was passing quickly and we were getting close to the beginning of November 1941. The maneuvers were about to end and both men and equipment showed the wear and tear; as well, our presence would leave its mark on Louisiana. It really was quite an experience: we learned a lot; caught all kinds of hell from the weather, humidity and swamps; and performed a lot of hard work.

It took some time to gather ourselves up in order to get ready for the return trip to El Paso. And we needed the rest. The 1,200 miles back to El Paso seemed like a million. Our equipment was all beaten up as were we, but we were going back different men. We were now molded into strong, experienced soldiers and knew what was expected of us. The best thing of all was that each of us now knew that we could and would live up to the army's expectations. Even after all of that I still loved the service and I believe Ernie and Frank were as excited as I was because of all that had happened to us. All the men were glad and anxious to get back to Fort Bliss; the trip took us about a week.

Somewhere along the way I made the grade of corporal. I believe it was just prior to the commencement of the maneuvers, at which time I had been in the army eight months. Through it all somehow I had this love for the service. It taught me so many good things, difficult things that helped to make me into a man because I was now able to cope with psychological and physical discomforts, and do it well. I thought further then about being an officer and what it would mean, and how hard I would have to work and the responsibilities to always do the right thing. And if you made a mistake, you always caught hell from the higher-ups. My decision not to proceed with officer training still lingered . . .

Dad took this photo of his buddies clowning around in the white sand dunes of New Mexico. My father's service album photo.

PART FIVE

DECEMBER 1941– MARCH 1942

Attack on Pearl Harbor Changes Everything and
the Course of My Life to Follow

Japanese bombing of Pearl Harbor, specifically Battleship Row at the beginning of the attack on the island of Oahu, December 7, 1941. Official Navy photograph NH 50930; public domain.

CHAPTER FOURTEEN

Our convoy returned to Fort Bliss around the twentieth of November; unknown to us, this was just weeks before the war with Japan was to break out. Rumors always seemed to get to the troops; those rumors reflected a lot of things that were currently going on diplomatically between the United States and Japan. The United States had stopped shipping to Japan tons of old cars and oil, both commodities of which Japan was in need. At the same time Japan was conquering other countries in the Far East and lots of war stories were created, some of which, when you were nineteen years old, just washed out and became not real. There seemed to be more important things to do like to get our passes to go to El Paso or possibly Juarez, and really put to use some of our crazy experiences that we had learned while in Louisiana, like being with women of ill repute.

Toward the end of November 1941 some of the rumors really came true, some did not. There were rumors that had us going to California, others off to the Philippines. It seemed our Louisiana convoy had barely unloaded our equipment when word came down that we were to start packing our three-inch guns and all equipment, including radar, searchlights, and everything else, to make ready to board a train that was evidently waiting for us to load all our trucks. Talk about lots of activity—rushing, all the time rushing to get ready day and night. Unfortunately, I got very ill with a terrible cold and sore throat along with a 102-degree temperature. In my delirium I was placed in the hospital at Fort Bliss and after coming out of it ended up staying for a few days more.

At the end of November the packing was at a fever pitch to load the train. I missed some of the hard work, but in the air I could feel the anxiety about something all around me. The first sergeant came around December 2 to check on me and to see how I was. As patients in the infirmary were being visited, there was some urgency in their inquiries with visitors as the diplomatic activities between Japan and the United States were the talk of the hospital. One could overhear visitors say things about the news and all of the activity at Fort Bliss, which only added to the anxiousness of the tone of the conversations. Sergeant Arbelo stopped by to see me and told me that our battery would be ready to leave very soon, and he asked me how I felt, encouraging me to get well as soon as possible.

One day led to the next and on December 7, 1941, in the morning the excitement was that the Japanese had just attacked Pearl Harbor. At the time that did not mean a hell of a lot to me because along with many other men, I had no idea where Pearl Harbor was. Some guys said it must be in the Philippines because the Japanese had been raising hell in that part of the world. Then the rumors about us going to the Philippines made sense; that was why we were going there. Well, somehow in the hospital there were a couple of sick guys who had been stationed in Hawaii, and they said that Pearl Harbor was a large naval base there. All of us patients then suddenly realized and understood the significance

Attack on Pearl Harbor Changes Everything

of where the Japanese had attacked our forces and what it meant for all of us as soldiers.

By the end of that day such significant world events had happened that everybody was excited and getting ready to go fight the "Japs" as they were called at that time. The following day President Roosevelt spoke and the hospital put the speech on the radio for all the wards to hear. He spoke about the day of infamy and that the Empire of Japan had attacked us and had caused tremendous damage to the naval units stationed in Pearl Harbor. He stated we had suffered a lot of casualties to our naval personnel, that the Japanese had used hundreds of airplanes brought to Hawaii by their aircraft carriers, and that a state of war would now exist between the United States and the Empire of Japan. That meant all troop movements had to be put into high gear, all personnel had to be gathered, and no matter where you were, hospital or otherwise, you had to be prepared to leave when your orders came.

Well, now the rumors were really flying and it all meant more rumors. Whatever they indicated, we all knew that army personnel would be headed someplace. San Francisco was the most talked about. All of our equipment was already gone as it had left Fort Bliss days before, and all that remained were troop trains and baggage. It was rumored that in San Francisco ships were waiting for us. There was a lot of excitement and everybody was pumped up and ready for whatever came. After all, who the hell did the country of Japan think it was? The country was not large, it had to depend on the import of raw materials from other countries, the Japanese soldiers were small, and all they ate was fish and rice. And besides, they couldn't see very well because their eyes were slanted. Such was the mentality of our soldiers at that time. Little did we realize that Japanese air, naval, and armed forces would become a respected and formidable foe throughout the entire war in the Pacific.

I guess my unit must have missed the rumor that we were not stopping in San Francisco. The Japanese had invaded and would eventually overrun the Philippines, but American forces would not be going back there until later in the war. Our 63rd Coast Artillery Batteries instead traveled on a train for five days and arrived on a rainy night in Seattle, Washington, on December 23 or 24, 1941. It was raining like it would never stop. The personnel and all their gear were unloaded from the train, and since all our equipment arrived ahead of us, and had been parked in what eventually became the King Dome sports arena grounds, the main goal was to get organized and put ourselves in order so that this army could implement all we had been trained to do. There were trucks to load, equipment to hitch together, and a checklist of items to complete in order to get ready to move.

As we all went about the business of preparing to depart, men were pumped up and excited to be someplace we'd never heard about nor been to before. Someone mentioned that we were in the Puget Sound area but that didn't mean anything to me. Once our gun crews were all gathered and loaded onto trucks, we departed for a destination called Beacon Hill. This area had been reserved for us in advance by army personnel who identified ideal areas for gun emplacements within the city of Seattle. When the convoy left the train station, to the west we saw these large objects all lit up. Blackouts had become a common practice at night, so I thought that these were trains because nothing was visible due to the rain.

Once arriving at our Beacon Hill staging area, the first task at hand was to set up camp. And because the army travels on its stomach, we had to put up the mess hall tents and stoves under the direction of Sergeant Smith—"Smitty," we called him. It took everybody to accomplish this effort because it was a huge job; all our training was paying off. Amazing how well a group of men that has been taught to work together can work like a well-oiled machine. Nobody talked back and there was no room to be tired, exhausted, or wet. You just pitched right in and got the job done. Now came the issuing of meal or C rations, prepared food in a tin. By now we were so hungry that everything tasted like filet mignon, real good, rain and all. Very soon though the kitchen crew would start the stoves, and maybe in the next few days we would enjoy a hot meal.

After erecting the mess tents and consuming our rations, we then proceeded to put up the troop tents. There was no way one could find a dry spot, so up the tents went on mud or whatever. Our duffel bags were wet and I don't remember if we had cots or not that first night, but I do remember that when we did eventually get cots, the legs sank into the mud, and the rain never stopped. Daylight came and we then had to set up our gun emplacements in an area that by now we determined to be a residential neighborhood. People would drop by to see us work and I guess they were as surprised to see us as we were them.

Putting up our gun batteries was no small task as we had to dig revetments for placing the guns and for storing our ammunition. This took up a hell of a lot of space in order to do so. After the camp was sort of settled, we next had to make the grounds as orderly as possible. This was also quite a job because the rain never stopped and the mud just got deeper. Finally all the equipment and camp were in order and our new home was finished.

All of this time the battery commander and the other officers and noncommissioned officers had the gun crews and radar equipment operating. We were ready for action if it came. There were a lot of planes flying overhead because, as we soon learned, the Boeing aircraft plant was located just to the west of us in the valley below Beacon Hill. By day this plant was all surrounded by barrage balloons and at night by our searchlights and gun crews primed for action.

One thing that I've always remembered was that on that first night we arrived in Seattle, as our convoys were going up to Beacon Hill, I could see a great expanse of blackness, and on this blackness were moving lights of something and I could not imagine what they might be. As I soon observed in daylight, these were the ferries going to Bremerton or elsewhere on Elliott Bay and Puget Sound, not trains as I had thought earlier. The only ferries we knew about were the Fairy Godmother or just plain fairies or queers, as they were thought of and referred to in those times, but here in Seattle they had ferries on the water. What a world, learned something new every day.

At the time I had no idea that Puget Sound was such a large body of water. As far as I was concerned, the only body of water had to be the ocean. It was sure something to see such a site as Puget Sound from Beacon Hill; such a large expanse of water and so close to the city of Seattle. Many of us had never seen anything like this vista, and it enabled us to observe so many new things that many of us were seeing for the first time, such as the barrage balloons, hundreds of them all over Boeing, just protecting the air space above the plant. How impressive it was! And Seattle, my, it was big, really big to us men from small towns. It seemed as though this city was scattered over a large territory.

After we had settled on Beacon Hill, the army was reorganizing its defenses and we were asked to move to another part of

Attack on Pearl Harbor Changes Everything

Seattle. This time we were moved to Youngstown over by West Seattle across Elliott Bay. All of the moving was done in the daytime, and to get to Youngstown, we had to go past the Boeing Plant on Marginal Way and Highway 99. As we went past Boeing, it was very busy as there were a lot of planes on the field though the plant was really quite small, just a few buildings and a little corporate office. I had never seen so many airplanes, cars, and people all together. Our drive to our new location was most exciting because of all the activity caused by our convoys. At that time there seemed to be a lot of army activity wherever you went in the city.

Upon our arrival at our new location, we determined that the area was a large city park located right on Delridge Way called Delridge Playfield, just across the street from Cooper Elementary School. I believe the school building remains, but I'm not sure it still functions as one. This park had beautiful lawns and trees and thank God, no mud! Our battery soon took the area over as we began to set up our camp and ready our equipment. Soon we would have our home again. All of us quickly understood that this area was also located within a residential neighborhood, with houses on residential streets, occupied by working-class people raising families. Some of these families I am sure had sons also in uniform or soon to be.

Typically the very first equipment that goes up is the mess tent or kitchen. Well, our Mess Sergeant Smitty was your standard mess sergeant. He was short and fat, Irish, a heavy drinker, and a hell of a good mess sergeant. When something was needed, he could always get it. Smitty knew how to play it to the hilt. The army, of course, had lots of food even though there was a food-rationing program for the civilians at that time. Whatever the army needed, they could get, including butter, meat, sugar, and flour. However, the civilians had the money to buy whiskey, and they also knew where and how to get it. Well, Smitty found that out right away as he liked whiskey, so he would barter with the neighboring civilians with his supply of foodstuffs. Of course, the old-timers in the battery, the sergeants and old soldiers, were good friends with Smitty, so they had plenty to drink as well.

Sometimes, however, the liquor supply would dry up and the ones who needed a drink did other things to quench their thirst. Supply Sergeant Galloway had his own system for such emergencies. The army supplied us with aftershave skin bracer and liquid shoe polish, both of which contain alcohol. Sergeant Galloway would drink the aftershave and strain the shoe polish to get what alcohol there was so he could survive the alcoholic tremors or DTs. There were all kinds and types of men in the army, so there were many things that people did that seemed strange to me. Bottom line, though, was that we were all in this war together and our purpose was to fight and win it.

The location of our battery within a residential neighborhood provided a source of curiosity to those civilians living nearby, as well as to us soldiers observing the homes and everyday lives of the citizenry. They watched us and we watched them. Across the street from our camp were typical, older homes with yards, cars, and young girls. One particular neighbor, a young lady about nineteen or twenty years old, was very well endowed, really well endowed! She would parade her large breasts while walking on the sidewalk on her side of the street. She had the largest pair I had ever seen. She knew damn well we soldiers were looking at her and she enjoyed us doing so. There were no catcalls, whistles, or verbal remarks from the men, as one tried to be as inconspicuous as possible while observing her. We didn't line up on the sidewalk, but the men all peeked at her as best we could. Such entertainment was beyond our reach, but she enjoyed it as much as we did. There was a mom-and-pop corner grocery store close by, so she went there quite often.

Our neighbors were nice folks and they went about their lives and doing all the normal things that have to be done in maintaining their households. Likewise we went on about our duties, doing all that was needed to be done to be ready for any emergencies or war-related battle activity. Our battery had been at the park for some time, one or two months, and was alerted to make ready to relocate up on a hill overlooking Boeing Field. This particular hill was called Pigeon Point and was a very good defensive position from which to carry out our responsibility of protecting Boeing aircraft manufacturing of the B-17 Flying Fortresses that performed so well in Europe for our country. So we once again had to dismantle our position at the Delridge Way city park location and make ready to move. At that time we were sort of advised that this next move would most likely be our permanent location. Nowadays this hill site is the location of South Seattle Community College.

By now it was late February or early March 1942. The news from the war in the Philippines was not very good as our armed forces were struggling against the Japanese and perhaps losing at that point. The hope was not good for saving that part of the world. The excitement and reality of the war was touching everybody, civilians as well as the armed forces. At that time in the conflict nobody thought that this could go on for three and a half more years.

Moving to the new location this time was a little more controlled because now we had to prepare a more permanent site. Everything we did was more thorough and by the book as we were to be seriously inspected by headquarters. Everyone was restricted to camp; nobody went off base unless authorized to do so by the battery commander. The only personnel who were allowed to leave were picking up essential supplies or ammunition for our guns to keep our battery operating.

For once we're digging in for the long haul. At our new location tents were made ready with wooden floors, everything was constructed to last, and the training never stopped. Overseas the war news was still not good as we were losing our asses in the Pacific. Both Bataan and Corregidor were on the verge of captivity, and nobody seemed to be able to help General Douglas MacArthur, who was in charge of the Philippine armies. He secretly had to escape by sea and traveled to Australia, where he began to rebuild his forces.

Our training got more intense and longer as the army doesn't know an eight-hour day. We worked as long as it took to prepare our defensive positions as the weeks went flying by and life began to become a little more routine once again. A mess hall and a recreation center were built from lumber that came from the Boeing plant below us. We would send two or three trucks down to recover the wooden propeller cases that were discarded in great numbers by Boeing, as they were building hundreds of B-17 Flying Fortress bombers that had four engines. Both the mess hall and the recreation center still stand to this day as someone made a private residence out of them!

By the end of six or seven months we were pretty well settled, and even though our duties never diminished, we began to relax a little. Passes once again were being issued and some guys, including yours truly, were sneaking out at night. There was a tavern on Delridge Way just west down the hill from our camp. This tavern is still there. At that time we had to walk down and back up a couple of steep hills on an unmarked trail and negotiate a path in the dark—a good place to fall and break a limb! But when one got to the tavern, nothing else mattered. A lot of the times when we snuck down there, no one had to buy a beer because the civilians would treat us as they were making lots of money and we soldiers were not. The trip down to the tavern also obligated you to bring back something for your peers. And since the Military Police, MPs, patrolled the area, you could not remain long and party at the tavern. If you were caught, you were returned to camp and reported to the battery commander, after which you ended up in the brig. And you can imagine what that meant to your ass! Consequently, we were always careful as we had a spotter outside of the tavern and the unmarked trail led to a nearby wooded area in which to hide.

One time I was down on a sneaker pass and my buddies up at camp were anticipating that I would bring them beer or wine from the bar. As this was a small tavern, sometimes not many people would be there at night. This particular time my friend and I entered the tavern; it was almost empty. The bartender always had a large wire basket filled with hard-boiled eggs placed on the bar countertop. My friend watched for MPs, and I went inside and bought some beer. There was a new bartender on duty, an old woman. My friend stuck his head in the door and told me that the MPs had just passed by and that we had better get the hell out of there. I had the beer in my hands, and as the old woman went to the back for something, I walked out with the basket of eggs to go with the beer. Since I had only paid for the beer, I ran like hell to the trail with my buddy. I don't know whether she ever missed the eggs or not. Anyway, all of us enjoyed the beer and eggs once we two returned to camp.

Time kept marching on and around March or April of 1942 the battery was short of manpower, so the reserves started flowing into the camp. We received about five or six reservists, all noncommissioned officers, sergeants, or corporals. All were old soldiers if not in time then certainly in experience as some had served in the Philippines and Hawaii, and at least one had served in China. They all had one or two patches on their sleeves, they demanded respect, they also had their own tent, and they pretty much did what they wanted until Sergeant Arbelo got on their asses. Al Moseley was one of these reservists and he seemed to be the only one with whom a person could talk. He and I became good friends soon after his arrival. These new men became a big part of our battery and soon they became one of us. They were what we called regular army and that seemed to set them apart from the enlistees and draftees.

Moseley learned his way around and became aware of the trail to Delridge Way and used it quite frequently, so much so that he met a girl who lived close to the trail just one block down from our camp. Her name was Lucille and they struck up a relationship, a very meaningful one. Over time, as they built on that relationship, their plans included marriage. However, at the time we both were still single and when we could get passes, we would most likely cat around a few miles south on Delridge Way in White Center where the night action was. To this day White Center is still colloquially known as RAT City. Probably because at that time it was referred to as the Reserve Army Training Center, or perhaps because some areas were designated Restricted Alcohol Territory.

Nonetheless, it seemed that White Center had a tavern on every corner, with lots of women, some of whom had boyfriends or husbands in the army but not close by. In other words they were available. So the soldiers went there for action. Lots of soldiers and ladies and not too many male civilians. There was a lot of whoopee being made there—a party town where anything goes. A couple of bucks would buy you a good time; beer was five or ten cents a glass and you could get into a dance hall for twenty-five or fifty cents. The downside was that the town was heavily patrolled by multiple Military Police.

There was also a policeman in White Center at that time named Horace; he must have been six foot ten and 275 pounds, I would guess. He didn't take too much crap from the soldiers, and if he thought you were disrupting the establishment, he would pick you up by the nape of the neck and throw you out. He could really do that! So in the process of your evening fun, you had to watch out for old Horace.

Boeing Field. This photograph was taken sometime in late 1943 or thereafter as the row of B-17Gs were not built until that time as a result of the ongoing learning curve for improvements to earlier B-17 Flying Fortress models. Note the nose turret gun that distinguishes the "G" models, in addition to other improvements made to this timeless war hero. The four engines per plane provided lots of wood for building facilities per my father's recollection. Photo courtesy of Boeing Historical Archives.

Attack on Pearl Harbor Changes Everything

This photo of Mike's Tavern and Cottage Grove Grocery appears to have been taken prior to WWII. This location was not quite three-quarters of a mile directly west of the 63rd Coastal Artillery encampment from which the soldiers, including my father, would sneak down to this tavern to tip a few or carry back to share with buddies at the base. Photo courtesy of Puget Sound Regional Archives, Washington State.

Downtown White Center during or just after the end of WWII given the production years of the vehicles. Given the numerous automobiles, it appears that this city was remaining active with people and business was booming. Photo courtesy of West Seattle Historical Society.

Boeing Field during the war years with barrage balloons and production facility rooftops camouflaged as residential streets and neighborhoods. Photograph courtesy of Boeing Historical Archives.

Attack on Pearl Harbor Changes Everything

Boeing workforce during WWII. In the background is the location of Beacon Hill where the 63rd Coast Artillery first dug in their protective defenses and encampment when first arriving in Seattle in late December of 1941. Photo courtesy of Boeing Historical Archives.

PART SIX

APRIL 1942– SPRING 1944

A Blind Date Leads To Marriage and
A Life That Grounds Me

My mother, Janet, is standing in front and her dear friend Lucille behind her. In all likelihood this photo was taken of the two West Seattle high school girlfriends in 1941 or 1942. Lucille and her boyfriend Al Moseley, my father's army buddy, introduced my mom to my father on a blind date in April of 1942. Lucille and Al Moseley married in June 1942. These two women remained friends for the rest of their lives. Image from my mom's photo album.

CHAPTER FIFTEEN

Al Moseley's girlfriend, Lucille, went to West Seattle High School. She had a very close friend and they would have girl talk about Lucille's experiences and the men at the battery. More girl talk led to Lucille mentioning to Al that she had a girlfriend who might be interested in a blind date or a double date with the two of them. Al asked me if I would like to meet one of Lucille's girlfriends, and I said sure I would be glad to as he seemed to be most happy with Lucille. That is how I met your mother, Janet Humphreys, who just happened to live quite close to the Delridge Way City Park where my unit had been temporarily stationed for a few months. She was one of our neighbors as she lived just about two blocks from our location at that time. What a small world.

I was nineteen years old when I met Janet. She was a lovely, redheaded seventeen-year-old girl, kind of shy but so was I. Upon meeting, we seemed to like each other, and we talked and laughed as there was no partying because I had very little money. I learned that Janet was one in a family of seven that was run by her father, Nicholas Humphreys, age sixty at the time. Since Janet's mother, Violet, had passed away in 1936 at age thirty-nine, Janet's father continued to run the household and maintain a tight ship at home.

She had two sisters, Violet, twenty-one, and Beverly, fifteen, and four brothers, including Edward, twenty, Jack, twelve, Charles, ten, and Calvin, eight. This family was very poor but very proper and lived in a rented, small two-story house quite typical of their neighborhood. Janet was a West Seattle High School student completing her junior year.

Lucille and Al got married in June of 1942 and that left Janet and I to continue dating one another. I found that I could relate to this nice girl who came from a large family that had to struggle to make a life with such little money. They had a respectable family life and I liked that, especially when I considered my own background and struggles. This young lady was a principled person who had a wonderful attitude about living. She was sincere and easy to get along with, and she accepted me for what I was, a soldier who really didn't have a lot to offer someone. Our relationship grew and we continued to build on it. I met Janet's family and her father liked me and trusted me to be a young man of principle. After all, I had very little typical experience as a child growing up, with no stable family life, and had lacked the parenting Nicholas was providing to his family. Janet was a person to be respected, and although she was poor, I believe life experience had made her a very compassionate and understanding person.

She and I continued to see each other and became closer in our thinking about a more permanent arrangement. After meeting her whole family, I felt good because these folks were real; all the kids respected their old man, there was a lot of happiness in that little house, and these were just plain, good folks. Her dad took to me from the start and I liked him because he was so ordinary. Nicholas liked to cook and he liked his beer, rye bread, and Limburger cheese. Whew! That was a pretty ripe cheese, but I learned to like it as it tasted a lot better than it smelled. All in all, it was a real treat to meet the whole family. I believe Janet's younger brothers and sister were excited about meeting a soldier. These kids were full of hell but only in a fun way, nothing mean.

In April or May of 1942 Janet and I became real close with each other. Somehow to me, at that time, she was the most important person in my life. The silly things that go through one's mind when things look like it might be a serious relationship: How does a soldier support a wife? Where does the money come from? Am I really ready to take on the responsibility of a wife? We had not really talked about it, but it looked and felt like we were falling in love. Of course, Janet was a respectable woman and I would not try to get too passionate with her even though we were both healthy and young and our hormones were jumping. In spite of being young, we seemed to have our heads on straight and were careful not to let anything happen that would put our feelings in trouble.

There were so many things we had to learn about each other, like, "How does one best make a family?" and "How ready are you really to assume those kinds of responsibilities?" Janet and I sincerely discussed how we felt about getting married; after all, there was a war on and she was still going to high school and I could not be with her all of the time. I wondered many times whether each of us really grasped all the realities that we would confront with such a decision. Well, we decided to get married, and I asked her father for her hand while he and I were eating rye bread and Limburger cheese. Nicholas said yes! Janet and I were both so very excited that we had done everything right and we set August 1, 1942, as our wedding date.

What should we do now? How much money could we save together for this wedding, twenty-five or forty dollars, maybe less? Who knew at the time? The month of August would come quickly and I guess she and I didn't have any idea of what was about to happen. We just had a date to be married and all the wedding preparations to make by ourselves. There were no parents scurrying about to make plans or anybody trying to put money together for us. Janet's sister Violet tried to help out as best she could, though Janet's father was no help whatsoever. Janet's grandmother living in Auburn was of little help to the effort as well. I guess Janet and I must have imagined that together we would just do the best we could, so that's what we did: proceeded with our plans even though we knew so very little. She and I could think for ourselves, but we just did not realize the scope of all possible considerations to be made. You never saw two more confused young adults in your life. Perhaps we were blessed in our own naïveté and that allowed us to do only what was needed and necessary. At the time, since my place was in the army, we always thought that Janet would stay at her home after we were married.

As one day followed the next before we knew it the time was August 1, 1942. I still don't remember how we decided to get married in Pierce County, Tacoma, Washington. I didn't know anything about Tacoma; we must have gone to the Pierce County Courthouse before getting married to obtain the marriage license. Tacoma was thirty miles away and in those years thirty miles was a long way in an old 1929 Model A Ford. Well, the day came and we all piled into the old Ford: Janet, her father, and sisters Violet and Beverly. Since Violet and her dad were not small people, the car was very well packed. But it didn't matter because Janet and I were excited about what was about to happen, with no plans beyond the wedding vows to be performed by the Pierce County Justice of the Peace. I believe that Al and Lucille were our best man and bridesmaid. I really can't remember, but it makes sense as they had introduced me to Janet, and as couples we still palled around together.

On our wedding day I do remember it was about midday, bright and sunny, and that my bride looked beautiful. I was scared as I thought to myself, "Well, what do we do now?" I never thought that we could not make it together; I just wondered how well I was going to handle it. After the wedding we drove back to Seattle to Janet's house, and I believe that there was a cake and we had a festive family atmosphere. All of the kids were excited and some neighbor friends of Janet's came over and joined us for a very happy time.

I knew we must have a honeymoon, but I didn't know where to go and money was ever so limited. But the idea came to me that we needed to go somewhere for dinner and celebrate. How we ever decided to go to Issaquah for dinner, I'll never know. Issaquah was a long way and we only had a couple of dollars for gassing the old Ford. But away we went and we found a little Italian restaurant and had dinner and visited together, which I am sure we enjoyed. We were now husband and wife, though neither one of us very experienced about what to expect. After our cozy dinner we headed back to Seattle for our honeymoon experience.

During the war years in Seattle it was not easy to find lodging, but we managed to find the Elliott Hotel in which to stay on 1st Avenue and Pike Street. The old building is still there and now is the Green Tortoise Hostel. I recall that we paid two dollars a night for a room looking out to the west at Pike Place Market. We were given a room upstairs, which became our honeymoon paradise, and we did what all honeymooners do. The both of us knew that there was something special about our communion and that we would seriously try to have a good life together. Boy, those are really special moments and emotional too for me all these years later. Janet and I were good together.

Since Pike Place Market was close by, there was a lot of foot traffic during the night, mostly service men exploring the town. In the morning we got up and had breakfast in a small restaurant in the market, and since I had only a three-day pass, we just squeezed in what we could to use up our short time together. I believe that we stayed only one night at the hotel because we did not have a lot of money so we couldn't continue to remain in the hotel and still be going to restaurants. I recall that we went back to Janet's house, seriously entranced in our own sense of being in love with one another. Come what may, hardships and otherwise, we had each other. It's very emotional for me to think back about those years, and to remember everything is not easy. It has been fifty-four years and so much life has been lived since that time.

I now was part of this family that had not much hope of ever being anything but poor. I believe Edward and Violet, Janet's two oldest siblings, might have worked and made a little money that helped with the house expenses. But when you only make thirty-five cents an hour, how much can that help? I do believe, however, that three square meals a day were served in that house and the food had to come from someplace. I am sure that whatever money I was able to provide to Janet must have helped, but it wasn't much. I can't remember what my pay was at that time; I think it was about thirty-five dollars a month. Not a lot of money but in those days it was not bad pay. Besides, Janet stayed at home with her family for a few months, so we had no rent to pay for the time being, though we did help with her family household expenses.

A Blind Date Leads to Marriage

Janet was always very considerate about helping her father, who I believe received some kind of state welfare. He wasn't employable due to a work-related accident he suffered around the time Janet's mother and new child passed away, and he had seven kids to support. Instead, her father worked about the house, went to the store, and did the shopping and the cooking. Nicholas was ever so good to Janet and the other kids, so I was happy to have her continue to live at home. I think about us as it used to be, with memories of ourselves still quite young and trying to be responsible and accept the obligations that come with marriage. She and I struggled with our ideas of gifts or loving gestures we wanted to give or do for each other, but we had a real money shortage. On the other hand, we were not in debt to anyone.

The army was the controlling part of my life, and so I was not home very often. Our battery used to travel to Yakima in eastern Washington for maneuvers and training. We could be gone for a month or six weeks at a time, but I never worried about Janet because she was home. As time passed, in the Fall of 1942, Janet and I were excited to find out that we were going to have a family. About that time the war had been ongoing for almost a year. In early 1943 Janet's family had to move and relocated to 706 Dearborn Street in downtown Seattle. Because places to rent were hard to come by, I believe the welfare office found this place located near Chinatown, a long way from West Seattle and Pigeon Point. This single-story, brick rental had been an old store, so it was quite large. The building was only recently razed this year for reconstruction into some other use.

After Janet's father and siblings moved, through some friends helping out, she found a basement apartment to rent in a home. This rental was located south of Seattle in what is now known as Burien, near Three Tree Point on Maplewild Avenue in a nice neighborhood close to Puget Sound. I believe that the rent was very reasonable and her landlords were very nice to her.

The first time I went to visit Janet, I had a very hard time trying to get there because her apartment was a long way from Burien, and that's where the bus stopped. I had been in Yakima for about six weeks, so Janet's moving took place in my absence. From the bus stop I had to walk to the house and I did not know the area, and even though I had an address, I had no idea where it was. I can't remember the details, but I finally found the house and I met the people where Janet was living. They let me in and told me that Janet was currently in the kitchen that they shared with her, as her basement apartment had none.

When I saw Janet, she was just beginning to show with Dick Jr. She was so surprised and happy to see me; I was most happy also, and the fact that she was starting to show with our child was a very exciting sight for me. This was an image unequal to any other life experience—unbelievable. And to think that we were just kids on unsure footing with what was to come. All of a sudden I realized the fantastic feeling and happiness in our becoming a family. Janet looked so beautiful with her red hair and wearing an apron; she was peeling potatoes and looked like a real housewife. I cannot explain the elation and pride that I felt when I thought, "Very soon we will have a baby," and I knew that Janet would be a good mother. I just hoped that I would be a good, responsible, and loving father, husband and provider to my family. Not having any frame of reference for such family matters, I knew that I was going to have some wonderful experiences, and I just trusted that I would live up to the job. Janet and I did not know anything about having children, but we'd both be happy with a boy or a girl. So as Janet's pregnancy progressed, the anticipation of our soon to be born child was very exciting to us both.

My first weekend at the house on Maplewild, Janet and I spent some time visiting with the man of the house, his wife, and their two children, getting to know one another. I believe he might have had an executive job at Boeing. I don't know for sure; I can't remember. Well, the next morning he gave me a ride back to camp in a beautiful La Salle automobile, a Cadillac, one very nice car. They must have had money, given the impressive car and nice house, at least Janet and I thought they were very well off.

Though I spent some more leave time there in the coming weeks, it was short-lived for us both. Unfortunately, in April of 1943 Janet's landlord had a personal family matter that made it necessary that she move back to the Seattle area; I just can't recall the actual reasons for this, but whatever it was, Janet had to relocate again. Instead of moving back in with her dad and siblings at the 706 Dearborn address, Janet contacted a friend from the old neighborhood in Youngstown and moved down the street to a house half a block from her previous residence. There she was given a private, upstairs bedroom. This provided us newlyweds with privacy that we would not have had living with Janet's family. The new room rental was in a home that had the same design and floor plan as where Janet's family had lived previously on this same street. Can't remember what the rent was, but I'm guessing it wasn't much. Janet stayed at this residence until just after she gave birth on July 16, 1943, to our son Dick Jr. Because he would require ongoing infant care from the Seattle Public Health Clinic located near her dad's Dearborn Street address, I helped to move Janet back there to be with her family. She and I went several times to this clinic throughout her pregnancy. Fortunately our trips became more convenient from the Dearborn Street address.

By this time Janet's immediate family had settled in at the Dearborn Street store living quarters. With the exception of its huge windows having to be covered with butcher paper, this old store took on the appearance of a home inside. Janet's father liked living at this location because it was close to Chinatown and he loved to play the Chinese lottery that he sometimes won. He also loved to eat Chinese noodles, pork noodles he called it. He got me into eating those noodles and I found that they were good. Old Nicholas did enjoy himself. There was an Italian bakery close by and he also loved going there to buy bread. I believe that sometime later Janet's younger brother Charlie got a job at that bakery.

What a joy and what a beautiful baby boy Dick Jr. was. Janet and I were so happy we didn't care that we had little money or that we lived in an old store apartment. She and I just knew we were a loving family, and all Janet's siblings and father were excited with this new little person now in the family. These are memories that will live forever in this old man's mind. They are all beautiful memories to me. It's hard to think back fifty-four years and imagine life as it really was then. There are some emotions here for me, a tear or two, but that was our life as I recall.

Sometime after we moved in with the family, Janet had to temporarily go stay with her grandmother, Janet Nelson-Peterson, living in a house located in the Auburn area. Janet's main purpose was to help her sister Violet with her newborn baby. Violet had sometime earlier met a soldier from Buffalo, New York, who was stationed at Fort Lewis just south of Tacoma. His name was Elmer, a kind and sincere man who was tall and looked like the Sergeant York in the movies. Eventually Violet and Elmer got married, and

A Blind Date Leads to Marriage

after their first child was born, and Violet was well enough to travel after staying with Janet and Dick Jr. at their grandmother's in Auburn, she moved to Elmer's hometown in New York.

After Violet left for Buffalo, Janet stayed at her grandmother's house for some time while her grandmother went back east to visit with family. Janet and Dick Jr. returned home to 706 Dearborn after being gone throughout the month of February 1944. I was so busy with army duties and responsibilities and travel to the Yakima firing range that our absence from one another was fairly routine. Our numerous letters to one another kept us warm and comforted, letters always bearing the acronym **S.W.A.K.** printed on the closing flap on back of the letter. **S**ealed **W**ith **A** **K**iss, for those readers too young to know or never exposed to World War II personal correspondence.

A couple of months after Janet returned from her grandmother's Auburn home, she and her dear friend Lucille decided to become roommates, so they set about searching for a rental house. I don't know how they found this house located in West Seattle on Ferry Avenue near Alki point. I suppose they thought it would be fun to live together and have a place to share with Al and me when we were able to go on leave. I remember Janet writing about all the hard work she and Lucille did with cleaning, painting, and fixing up the house with new curtains and such, and how happy and excited they were to finally move in at the end of April 1944. For the life of me I can't recall why this arrangement didn't last but three or four months. Janet, Dick Jr., and I ended up living there as a family after it became necessary for Lucille to move out for whatever reason.

This house was a great place to live, with a fantastic view of downtown Seattle and Puget Sound, though Seattle's skyline at that time was not quite what it is today. The house was furnished, so it suited us just fine. Another thing about the house was that it was located close to one of Janet's high school friends, Myrtle. This was convenient because I could not always be there and Janet having a good friend close by was very helpful, especially with the new baby. We also had Alki Beach nearby, and sometimes Al and Lucille would come over and we would all go dig butter clams at low tide, day or night, at the beaches located down the hill. We all loved those clams and they were so easy to gather.

Janet and I lived at the Ferry Avenue house for some time, and our lives were beginning to become and feel stable and routine. We were just starting to buy our own furniture and create our own hearth and home together. She and I were leading happy and satisfying lives, always getting along very well together, never fighting or arguing about simple things, so in that way our lives were blessed. Janet was such a great lady and she made our relatively poor home a rich one with her loving nature and the way she put up with me. She made our world complete and I just contributed a small part; she was that kind of woman. Somehow we felt that our lives were whole because we both had intimately known poverty and hard times. As for me, growing up I had never known a family life, so this experience was most enjoyable.

So often in life when happiness reigns, everything else is secondary. My wife and I always seemed to give each other our full support, so there was never any reason to have conflict in our relationship. Perhaps we were just dumb and poor in one way and rich in others. Or in looking back on it now, maybe we were mature beyond our years, having come up in life the way that we each did. The one thing that helped was we never had any serious financial obligations. Since we could not afford much, we kept our debts small so we could handle them.

A Blind Date Leads to Marriage

Our friendships were also changing as some of my army friends were transferred out on cadres that would come up occasionally; either they volunteered or were assigned to other duties. Ernie and Frank volunteered to serve on a merchant ship traveling from Alaska to Russia. Soldiers in the army were always subject to being assigned to a cadre that was going somewhere that needed our type of manpower. So though Janet and I had a life that had a lot of comfort, it was always understood to be tentative. I never volunteered to leave for a new assignment because I had a family, but if I had been assigned, of course, I would have gone.

My life in the army remained routine, but now I enjoyed just a little more freedom, so I was able to come home more often. By that time I had made corporal and was making fifty-six dollars a month. That was a hell of a lot of money to Janet and me, so financially it was easier to enjoy and afford our lives as a family of three. By now the war was in its third year, with fighting going strong in both Europe and in the Pacific. In some ways our armed forces were beginning to fight back and making some very good gains, while at home life remained on a war footing.

One day led to the next and then another, with the battery going to Yakima Firing Range three to four times a year to train on new guns and the latest equipment. Our outfit just stayed in Seattle during the peak of the war. Nationally there must have been thirteen to fifteen million persons in total from all the service branches and only two to three million service personnel actually overseas in the Pacific and Europe. Our batteries were the reserve forces just living our lives and waiting to be called to duty when needed elsewhere. Civilian life was very different from ours in the service, as the civilians seemed to have it pretty good, working long hours, making good money, and enjoying their lives as best they could.

After some time of this daily routine, soldiers started to sneak out at night to work in several defense plants throughout the Seattle area. All this was night work only because one still had their army responsibilities, so duty was first priority. At that time army personnel were not on high alert but always expected to be available to answer the call. There was a charcoal plant situated at the bottom of the hill below our camp at Pigeon Point. This provided an opportunity to make a few extra bucks; I believe it was common knowledge. The charcoal job left filthy, nasty, black dust all over every part of your body. The charcoal was for gas masks, which at that time were regular issue in the military. I also got a second job at Ferguson's Steel Foundry located on West Marginal Way. It was quite a distance from camp, but it paid a little more money because it was a dangerous place to work with hot and molten metal. I worked there for quite some time relative to my other civilian jobs, which enabled Janet and me to buy a little more of the things we needed at that time. I also learned more about the men who worked in such settings, as well as what hard work is really like, that your work can mold one's life, and that things are never handed down to you.

All of these extra jobs did not last too long for some personnel choosing to work because soldiers couldn't always be available to do a shift at the plants. And though the work was hard, those of us doing so certainly appreciated the opportunity to make the extra cash as it sure helped out. Eventually, as it turned out, sometime in 1944 protocols tightened up in the armed services for personnel being able to work in defense plant jobs.

A Blind Date Leads to Marriage

Rental home of the Humphreys family, 1941. You can imagine it must have been quite cozy with a family of eight living in this small house. Photo courtesy of Puget Sound Regional Archives, Washington State.

My parents' wedding day photo from a family album. I do not know where this photo was taken; my mom may have told me but it is long forgotten.

The Elliott Hotel located on the corner of 1st Avenue and Pike Street, directly across from the Pike Place Farmers' Market main entrance on 1st Avenue (My parents' honeymoon ste.). Today the building operates as the Green Tortoise Seattle Hostel on the second floor, with ground-level miscellaneous shops. Photo courtesy of City of Seattle Historical Archives.

The Humphrey's new 1943 address downtown Seattle at 706 Dearborn. The smaller portion of the building, address 704, continued to be occupied by a laundromat. Photo courtesy of Puget Sound Regional Archives, Washington State.

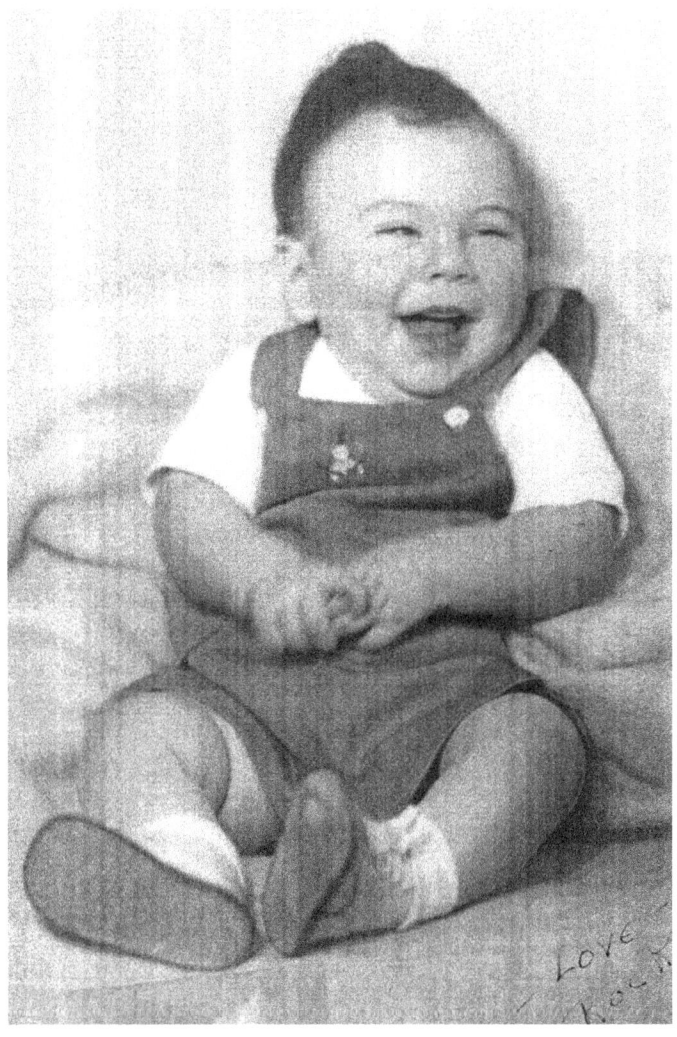

Dick Jr., affectionately nicknamed "Rocky" by his Uncle Jack. This stuck throughout his childhood years. Photo from mom's family album.

This is a 1943 Fort Lewis, Tacoma, Washinton, wedding photo of Violet, my mother's older sister, and her new husband, Elmer. Violet moved in 1944 to live with Elmer's family in Buffalo, New York. After the war ended, they remained on the East Coast and raised their family. Photo from mom's family album.

My mother's grandmother Janet Nelson-Peterson at home in Auburn, 1950.

A Blind Date Leads to Marriage

Ferry Avenue rental occupied by Mom and Lucille. After Lucille moved out, then both my parents and Dick Jr. lived here. The house faced east toward the city of Seattle and Elliott Bay. It is completely remodeled now and the setting is very different with large trees and numerous houses. Photo courtesy of Puget Sound Regional Archives, Washington State.

What the view resembled during the war years from the Ferry Avenue rental and from Harbor Avenue S.W. beaches. Photo courtesy of Museum of History and Industry (MOHI), Seattle, Washington.

A time period image of the above centered, multistory building in downtown Seattle that still stands today, though it was completely renovated during the late 1980s or early 1990s. When my father and mother lived at the nearby 706 Dearborn address, they came to this building to obtain pre- and postnatal care for my mother and Dick Jr. At that time, the Public Health Department was located in this facility, which fronts to the south on Yesler Way that runs east and west. I recall in the mid-1950s going with my parents to see my grandfather, Nicholas, who resided for a short time in the hotel located just across the street, left of center with the Smith Tower sprouting from the hotel roofline. My grandfather Nicholas passed away sometime later in 1957. Photo courtesy of Puget Sound Regional Archives, Washington State.

HUMPHREYS FAMILY PHOTOGRAPHS

Nicholas John Humphreys, my mother Janet's father, about thirty-six years of age; photo taken around 1919. Family photo album.

Violet Marguerite Humphreys, Janet's mother, about twenty-three years of age; photo taken same time as the previous image. Family photo album.

A Blind Date Leads to Marriage

Late 1945 photo with Dick Jr. two and a half years old, on his right Uncle Charlie, twelve, Uncle Jack, fourteen (behind Charlie), and Uncle Cal, ten, behind Dick Jr. All of Dick Jr.'s aunts and uncles, with the exceptions of Violet, who moved permanently to New York, and Edward, who went his own way in life, were an important part of Dick Jr.'s parents' lives, his life, and those of his future siblings, on a routine basis for many years yet to come. See next image for all of the children in 1936. Family photo album.

Family photo of my mother's family in or around 1936. The oldest, Violet, stands center in the background, to her left is Edward, born second, third is my mother, Janet, holding the family's youngest, Calvin, number seven, to Mom's left is Beverly, number four, on her left is Jack, number five, and Charles was the sixth, sitting on the pedestal at the far left.

MY FATHER'S SERVICE PHOTO ALBUM

My father's #4 Gun Crew members. This crew seems to have remained together throughout the war effort. Richard Hernández standing on the rear right. All of these following photos of his gun crew are from his army photo album.

The gun crew with their final base location at the Pigeon Point area of West Seattle overlooking Boeing Field, now the site of South Seattle Community College. My father is standing in the center of the image next to the breach of the gun, with a satchel of some sort under his left arm.

A Blind Date Leads to Marriage

I believe this photo is one of several that were taken at different times when the personnel had to travel to Eastern Washington for training in the desert area of the army's Yakima Firing Range. My father is sitting in the center on the gun.

Yakima Firing Range training for Dad's gun crew with new and improved weapons.

Dad, on the left, would never give me the details on this photo, but I always get a smile on my face when I look upon it. Maybe it was a different kind of Yakima Firing Range!

PART SEVEN

SUMMER 1944– NOVEMBER 1945

The Pacific War Intensifies and
Overseas Duty Calls Me

Army personnel loading troop carrier at the Port of Seattle Pier 5 (future Pier 56). The above photo documents the role of troop carrier LST-817 that ferried military personnel to the Pacific Theater prior to the invasion of Okinawa as identified in NavSource.com history for the ship.[4] The 63rd Coast Artillery Antiaircraft Batteries, along with numerous other army personnel, embarked from this same pier to participate in the invasion of the major island of Japan once the battle of Okinawa was finished and won by the United States and its Allies. Photo courtesy of the Port of Seattle Archives.

---

4   NavSource Naval History—Photo Archive Main Index: Ship images history, crew contacts, building, service, and final fate information.

CHAPTER SIXTEEN

In the summer of 1944 the army was receiving new equipment, and all battery personnel were expected to learn about using the very latest artillery pieces and radar. The war was getting more serious for the stateside armed services as preliminary War Department planning was being undertaken for the invasion of Japan. Based upon our forces' losses in the Pacific island-hopping campaign, it was anticipated that there would be an increasing number of men and materiel required to invade Japan. Tremendous losses were expected to occur as a result of the experiences our armed services had had to date, confronting the tenacious fighting abilities and mentality of the Japanese soldier. We troops hoped that we had received all the training necessary to be ready to face the enemy.

At home our lives were joyful. Dick Jr. was getting to be a little over a year old and we were able to do a little more as a family. Janet and I would visit with Grandpa often because she was always thoughtful about her dad and her brothers and sisters. Her family members seemed always to get along as Nicholas remained in charge of things and kept the house operating routinely and in order. As for my army life, nothing ever changed; one day was the same as the next.

During the summer of 1944, I was off for a few weeks and I got a job at the Rainier Brewery. Man, what a job that was with good pay but of short duration. It was a cold workplace because the temperature had to be kept low due to the beer products. My particular job was a dirty one as I had to climb on the inside of these giant, wooden beer-storage tanks, removing the smelly pitch and beer residue until it was all cleaned up. My boss worked the hell out of me, but I could stop and have a beer anytime. Nothing like cold draft beer—can't even feel the buzz when you've been sweating profusely. All these miscellaneous jobs helped to improve our lives as Janet and I now had a small sum of discretionary income. This enabled us to enjoy a few material things or eat a meal out once in a while.

As the war progressed and it became more certain that significant numbers of additional stateside troops would be going overseas, our training became more intense and trips to the Yakima Firing Center more frequent. Army life became my life as more and more soldiers found that our time was not ours. Janet and I still lived on Ferry Avenue in West Seattle, though as fall 1944 rolled around, more serious action was taking place in Europe and the Pacific. After discussing these matters and their implications on our lives, Janet and I decided it was best for her now to move back in with her dad at the old store on Dearborn. This was fine with me because I knew she would be safe there. So we moved back in with Grandad and the kids. We created our bedroom area by placing blankets on a heavy metal frame to serve as a privacy area for Janet and me and a nursery for Dick Jr.

Janet's father was the finest grandpa anybody would ever want; he also made the best sauerkraut and pork knuckles, dumplings, and all kinds of dishes. That was why my wife became such a good cook with ham and country gravy, turkey, and that good dressing she always made.

One item that Nicholas prepared and the family ate that tasted pretty good sticks out in my mind: horsemeat. There was an actual horsemeat market convenient to where we lived, where you could purchase Montana Cayuse horsemeat. For twenty-five or thirty cents one could buy a hell of a steak! I remember the long waiting lines outside this market. Now mind you, people had to have ration stamps for beef purchases and we used those as well if we had them, but the military always had priority for beef supplies.

Life for us was good at the Dearborn residence and we all enjoyed it! We continued to live our lives day to day, and Dick Jr. really seemed to be happy living in this environment. Grandpa had an old record player and our son just loved playing records and singing along, especially cowboy music by Bob Wills—yippee! He was such a cute little guy and a joy to both Janet and me. Life remained casual in the States even though war raged overseas.

As to how our gun batteries ever managed to stay in Seattle, I'll never know. It must have been the sheer number of military personnel available in the country at that time. As I mentioned before, there were only about two to three million personnel overseas, while the majority of our forces were stateside. However, in the spring of 1945 my time was to come. With our departure anticipated in the near future, we traveled to Yakima for final rehearsal and spent a lot of time completing intense drills and forced marches and familiarizing ourselves with newer, heavier guns and improved technology. Soon all of the preparations we had made were about to be put to good use.

In mid or late April of 1945 the 63rd Coast Artillery Batteries were transferred to Fort Lewis, south of Tacoma, and stayed there about two months, occupied with doing all the final preparations necessary before departing. I was able to come to Seattle I think two times to visit with my family before leaving the West Coast. Janet became pregnant with Sherry Lynn just before I left to go overseas. Being stationed at Fort Lewis was very exciting because it was a beehive of activity. Everybody there was busy preparing to leave the States, while at the same time, more troopers were still coming in up until about the last two weeks before we left. Nobody could call home or even write as everything was being censored; it was a complete lockdown. Our gun batteries then started packing to leave for Fort Lawton located north of the Magnolia neighborhood of Seattle. We stayed there for about a week.

All the while Janet knew that this was the way that it was going to be, so she expected and prepared for what was to come. She was comfortable staying with her father, and I was satisfied that she would be well taken care of by her family members. And though she was expecting our second child, she had her hands full with Dick Jr. and helping her dad with the housekeeping and her siblings; and life goes on. As for personnel in the military, we were constantly reminded that total secrecy was essential and that talking about our activity was forbidden. When we arrived at Fort Lawton, it was another beehive of activity with trucks coming and going around the clock.

Finally our turn came to depart early one morning. All personnel loaded up, everybody checked in, and we were on our way; it must have been late June or early July of 1945. Our convoy took us to Seattle waterfront's Pier 5 (future Pier 56), and there waiting for us was APA #26, USS *Samuel Chase*, a huge army attack transport that was to become our home for what seemed like a long time.

Overseas Duty Calls Me

(Unbeknownst to my father at the time, this ship had a storied past, having participated in invasions of North Africa, Sicily and Salerno in Italy, D-Day's Normandy Omaha Beach, and southern France.)[5]

At Pier 5 was an army band playing "Sentimental Journey," which was appropriate because we were all leaving our families and most of the things that meant home. Upon leaving the pier, there were people from the Red Cross and dockworkers all waving goodbye. On this transport there must have been well over a thousand troops plus whatever size the ship's crew was. Slowly we moved out of the dock and into Elliott Bay and out into Puget Sound, seeing the last of the Seattle skyline disappear, the houses getting smaller and smaller, and our thoughts were kind of sad. But after all, millions of soldiers have left loved ones and gone off to do their duty, with many never to come home. Somehow as you leave to go, the last thing a person thinks about is not coming back.

Through the Straits of Juan de Fuca we traveled, continuing to see the houses and mountains disappear after us, and the water began to get a little rougher and eventually one started to think about getting seasick. All of us anticipated that was coming and very soon! In the meantime the ship's captain was saying, "Now hear this," and he welcomed us aboard the ship and told everyone that we would be on board for quite some time, and that we would be observing war conditions when we entered into the open ocean. And also, because we were not accustomed to being aboard a ship, he said that some of us would probably experience some discomfort, but that it would pass shortly and then the trip would be more routine. He informed us that the ship's crew would assist

---
5 Ibid. USS Samuel Chase.

us in finding our way about the vessel, and that life jackets were to be either worn or within reach at all times.

As the day progressed, some fishing boats passed us, and they waved and tooted their horn because they could see that these were troops going someplace, so they wished us well. The Straits of Juan de Fuca are quite long and of course the ship was going slowly, which seemed so serene. You could feel the power of the engines as the propellers turned, and from the back or stern of the ship, you could see the wake that they left in the water as they took us away from home. Most of the troops were just seeing the blue water for the first time and a lot of us had never been aboard a ship. The water was calm and smooth with plenty of seagulls flying about the ship while it seemed to sway gently, and there was a sense of quiet as most of the troops were just leaning over the rail thinking of personal matters, mostly feeling melancholia and knowing that we were leaving another world behind. There was some nervous laughter and lots of smoking going on, then our officers started to assemble us and the battery commander gathered the non-coms, me included as a newly minted sergeant, to see that all the men found their assigned billets. That was some duty trying to find our billets or hammock and a place to be when not on deck.

The day was beginning to wear out and the sun was low on the horizon. It was a long time getting out of the straits, so by that time all troopers were settled in their billets, and knew where the head (toilet) was; they knew that starboard meant right side of the ship, port was the left, the bulkhead was the ship's wall, and the deck was the floor. Our first meal was C rations because there had not been enough time to prepare a shipboard meal, but better times were coming. As usual rumors were alive and well. The rumor as to why we took so long to travel out of the straits was that we were going to be part of a convoy and the other ships had to have time to get to an area just out of the straits.

Well, into the big ocean we now started our real journey, and of course the first thing that occurred was the ship found a big hole in the ocean and in we went. Surprise! This was it and this was the way it was going to be most of the trip. The ship started swaying to and fro just a short time after we had eaten our C rations, so all were primed to get seasick. Lo and behold, we did with a vengeance. It wasn't too long before the ship's railings were fully occupied with sick soldiers and sailors alike, as there were a lot of new seaman on board as well. I don't know of anything that makes a person feel as awful as seasickness.

The time was passing and all were getting used to being aboard ship as life began to become very routine. There was a lot of time to do almost anything, including playing cards, reading, sleeping, or once in a while getting seasick all over again. There were some orientation classes, mostly on ship safety and the use of the ship's facilities such as the store, taking showers with a water shortage, and personal hygiene. We also had to be careful of rats aboard ship, especially if you chose to sleep on deck at night when it was too hot below decks. The rats seemed to have an appetite for toenails, so we were warned to keep our shoes on. In fact, this did happen to some soldiers as rats nibbled on their toes while the soldiers were sleeping without shoes. We also did some training on maintenance of our equipment. By and large, though, life was very serene and quiet, just the swaying of the ship to and fro.

A few days out to sea, we came upon a large ship convoy, not physically close but well within our field of vision, that included some Liberty ships, Landing Ship Tanks (LSTs), and some destroyers; it was a busy ocean. By this time we were well out into open seas and one of the sights enjoyed were the dolphins and other fish that would come out of the water and fly several feet and then be gone—quite a diversion. At night everything was dark aboard ship topside, while in the rest of the ship only red lights lit the hallways. Also, as the vessel cut through the phosphorous in the water, the wake of the ship lit its sides as well as the wake. What a sight! This was most interesting to us landlubbers.

After several days out to sea the convoy had not made much progress as I believe that we could only travel as fast as the slowest ships in the convoy. I think that these ships were the LSTs, huge rectangle-shaped vessels that were of flat-bottomed and low-draft design for amphibious operations. They would unload tanks, tractors, trucks, and other large vehicles and equipment on the island beaches from the large drop-down door at the bow of the ship. The other thing that we learned after a few days was that the convoy had to travel in a zigzag pattern most of the time. This was done in order to make the ships more difficult targets for any enemy submarines in the area. Of course, after we were informed of the purpose of the zigzag strategy, we then took more notice of it and watched for it to occur; it got our attention. After several days out to sea, the ship became just another routine thing, one day leading to the next; it was truly a new experience.

While on the ship, the world news, especially war news, was broadcast over the public address (PA) system. There was also a small ship's newspaper that was published about twice a week that told all about world events. There was a hell of a lot of heavy fighting in the Pacific at that time, especially during our invasion of Okinawa that began April 1 and ended June 22, 1945, with many weeks of mopping-up operations to be completed. Having personally been there just days after the mopping-up ended, and inspected where some of the fighting had taken place and read subsequent accounts of our invasion, I can tell you that the Japanese had defended Okinawa with all they could, using the island terrain to their advantage, well camouflaged machine gun pillboxes, interconnected tunnel systems that concealed soldiers that fought to their deaths, heavy artillery firing from hidden hillside caves, and suicide planes attacking our naval ships at sea. Though we eventually won the battle, it was at a high cost of many wounded and dead Japanese and Americans.

Our ship and convoy were continuing to slowly approach the war zone. Then in early August 1945, we got the news over the PA system that the atomic bomb had been dropped on Hiroshima and that the casualties had been very heavy. But still a Japanese surrender was the last thing their military wanted to do.

By this time we had been at sea forever it seemed and finally we spotted the island of Eniwetok, a very small island maybe one mile in size, with white sand and hardly any palm trees or any other sign of vegetation. I understood that the highest point of the island was six feet above sea level. It actually took roughly forty-five days to arrive at this first stop, a very small island within the Marshall Island group. In hindsight, of course, we did not know where we were headed at that time, only that we were on our way to most likely invade the main island of Japan. As the convoy approached the island, we could see that there had been some kind of action here because there were a couple of ships that had been sunk or beached hulks. I believe that our ship just stopped there to reorganize the convoy and I suppose to prepare for any possible action. I don't recall that anybody went ashore here from our ship. However, it was relaxing just to be anchored for a couple of days, even though all of the activity by the ship's personnel indicated that they were getting ready for whatever was ahead of us.

After everything was reorganized with the convoy, it was time to set sail again, now toward where the war was taking place. We were alerted to be on the lookout for anything unusual. Finally the ship's captain announced over the PA system that the ship was preparing to get underway and slowly the ship started to move. There were a lot of vessels gathering, including destroyers, destroyer escorts, troop carriers, and LSTs, and we could see the convoy beginning to move forward. At this point on the map I would guess that we were 4,300 miles from the good old US of A.

A couple of days after we left Eniwetok, the news came over the PA system that a second atomic bomb had been dropped on Nagasaki; it was about the ninth of August, 1945. Then there was some talk of surrender so that appeared to pretty much do it for the Japanese, though there were remnants of isolated fighting still occurring. Our convoy was still some distance from Okinawa when the powers that be decided that the troops aboard ship needed a break. So the next island we came to, Ulithi Atoll, would be an ideal stop.

This was a beautiful island and looked so inviting with sandy beaches and lovely palm trees; it seemed like a paradise. However, there had been some battle activity here too. I believe some devastation was visible, maybe minor activity, but after spending so much time on board ship, it was most welcome to go ashore. There were several ships unloading troops for a little R&R. All of us had to disembark down a rope net to the landing craft but didn't mind as this was going to be a beer stop. Then a ride on the landing craft took us to the beach about two miles away. Once we reached the beach, there was already a canteen set up to pass out beer or pop, whatever you wanted. Just to stand on solid earth felt so good! You can imagine how a bunch of men felt after having been in a confined space for so long. We had a beer or two that was hot to drink; the buzz hits you more quickly than when cold, and with the hot sun blazing, it was a good one.

Once on the island we noticed that there were natives there, and they continued to go about their daily routines, climbing palm trees to get coconuts, even giving the troops some. We had fun trying to break these coconuts open without any hammers or machetes available. Noticing this, the natives showed us how to do it, and we enjoyed the taste of the milk and meat. We were allowed to spend several hours on Ulithi looking around, resting under palm trees, listening to the waves hit the beach, and we all seemed to have a little beer buzz going.

There were numerous soldiers on the beach because at that time several troop ships were anchored off shore. During the spring and early summer all of our armed forces' branches had been massing for US departure in preparation for the largest ever planned invasion of the islands surrounding Japan, and then the island of Japan itself. Each of us on Ulithi at that moment in time had a part to play in this massive assault had it actually been necessary to do so. Fortunately, for all military personnel and the populace on the home front, the war was just about over or soon would be. The Japanese Emperor, cabinet, and military heatedly debated over the unconditional surrender demanded from the United States and our Allies. Ultimately, Japanese decision makers finally accepted unconditional surrender on August 15, 1945, after which a formal truce was signed on the deck of the USS Missouri on September 2, 1945.

Finally, our short time on Ulithi Atoll came to an end, so it was back to the ship. We were still a ways from our final Okinawa destination. Though the war was about over, the convoy still had to take precautions from an enemy, who, operating submarines or aircraft, might still desire to continue fighting.

Period photo of Seattle Brewing & Malting Co. The "Rainier Brewery" where my father worked part-time to supplement family finances. Note the signage on top of the tallest building naming brands Rhienlander and below Rainier. Today Interstate 5 runs north and south on the east side or left, forested side of this photo. Courtesy of Puget Sound Regional Archives, Washington State.

Yes, it is true! Pike Place Market sold horse meat.
Courtesy of Seattle Now and Then.[6]

---
6 Horse Meat Anytime – J.R. Sherrard – Seattle Now and Then – February 27, 2010.

Two for You, One for Me

Time period photograph. Fort Lawton in Seattle's Magnolia neighborhood was a very busy place for soldiers to be stationed temporarily before disembarking overseas to fight the Japanese. Today this large area is called Discovery Park and provides a variety of outdoor recreational opportunities. Most recently, several of the remaining military command staff residential homes were remodeled and upgraded while keeping the original architectural style and design integrity. Land area, I presume, was allotted for these historical homes as a private residential neighborhood. The majority of these houses had million-dollar-plus asking prices. Image is courtesy of Museum of History and Industry, Seattle, Washington.

USS Samuel Chase at harbor somewhere in the Pacific or European war theaters. This was to become my father's home for the next several weeks as men and materiel traveled from Seattle to Okinawa for the invasion of Japan. Public domain photo courtesy of NavSource.org.

This beached LST photo shows the flat-bottom design and the loading/ unloading large bow doors of the vessel. The flat-bottom design was not conducive to smooth sailing in typhoons or hurricanes, both of which my father experiences later in the following pages. LST 325 was left high and dry on Normandy Beach at low tide on June 12, 1944. Public domain photo courtesy of NavSource.org.[7]

---

[7] NavSource Naval History – Photo Archive Main Index: Ship images history, crew contacts, building, service, and final fate information.

This 1945 photo is taken from Sorren Island, one of several islands within Ulithi Atoll. The view is to the north anchorage area within the atoll's expanse. United States Navy public domain photo.

CHAPTER SEVENTEEN

Just a few more days at sea and we finally arrived at Okinawa. What a tremendous ship armada! Since there was no particular military activity taking place on the beach where our ship arrived, we disembarked our transport; all the other vessels in our convoy, including the LSTs, unloaded all of the equipment, including trucks, guns, searchlights, numerous kinds of vehicles, supplies, and fuel—all that was necessary to equip and arm our coast artillery contingent.

It was a very hard job to get all of this equipment gathered up and get ready to report to a location that would be our staging area. Though the war was essentially over, there was still a possibility that sporadic fighting could occur. Our area was secured by posting guards, and there was so much activity that it made it quite confusing, even though there appeared to be no particular danger at hand. However, given the possibility of the enemy continuing to fight in the outlying islands isolated from mainstream Japan, we were prepared to defend ourselves as our rifles were to remain loaded and at the ready at all times.

The location where our war materiel was unloaded happened to be very close to Naha, the capital and main city on the southwest side of Okinawa. There was much devastation and ruin present here as there had been some real horrible, intense bombing, artillery shelling, and hand-to-hand fighting. All the buildings were damaged and the water and power were off.

Our unit finally got all of our equipment secured, and the next order of business was to get to our assigned area. We all marched in an easterly direction for maybe fifteen miles toward the other side of the island to arrive at our new operations base close to a smaller town that I believe was called Yonabaru. I believe there had been a Japanese base located in this area. We traveled through terrain that had seen some bitter fighting. There were dead Japanese soldiers by the sides of the road and tanks and trucks that were wrecked. In some of the foxholes by both road and hillsides were dead Japanese soldiers who had been fighting from those positions and were still standing up; some of them were burned to a crisp from flamethrowers. Very real acts of war had occurred here. Scary stuff!

All of this, of course, made our march on this road seem more dangerous. While marching, some of the men would observe a cave and just open fire with automatic rifles to eliminate the danger of Japanese soldiers, who might still remain in the caves, from firing on our column. One could hear some other sporadic fire in the hills close by. The deeper we walked into the hills to our position, the more leftovers of war were encountered: more bodies, more destroyed equipment, and more sporadic rifle fire. Maybe some of the marines and army troops were still hunting down elusive Japanese soldiers.

When we finally arrived at our intended base camp, tents had to go up and regular camp duties continued. My battery unit set up our equipment but just to keep us doing something. The war was now officially over; however, our action was just starting. Our particular troops were assigned the duty of policing Okinawa and the several smaller, outermost Japanese islands. This task was not going to be a piece of cake and possibly not really safe either. Once our duties were specifically detailed to us, there were a lot of lifted eyebrows and second looks. Our batteries were going to disarm Okinawa and surrounding islands, a goodly size job. So we started without delay to do just that.

On Okinawa the destruction of the island pretty much had taken care of any equipment that would have existed there prior to our arrival, as it had already been secured or destroyed. We began at Naha. There was not much left of this city due to the intensity of the fighting here. There were, however, a lot of houses that were still standing and a lot of civilians still there as well, maybe even some of which were Japanese soldiers, though not in uniform. These individuals were the men who could be dangerous. Our men had to go into these houses and do a real search for weapons and ask questions of these people. Mind you these were civilians, mostly people who were farmers and laboring folks, and we were soldiers, battle equipped, and looking very threatening to them. The Japanese common people were controlled by and worked for the Japanese military, so going through their homes and inspecting all of their possessions was scary to them and with good reason. These farmers were trying to get their lives reorganized and to continue making some kind of life for their families.

Upon completion of our responsibilities on Okinawa, the time came to then start securing the outer islands, as our extended duties called for us to do. In order to accomplish this, we had to board ships to get there. The troops were loaded onto LSTs and our adventures began. There were several ships to accommodate the contingent that would be undertaking this task. Our duties were to take all of the war equipment that was found—including planes, tanks, trucks, artillery, small arms, explosives and such—and load it all onto large barges to be dumped into the ocean. We also were to gather any remaining Japanese troops and put them into a guarded compound. There were not that many Japanese soldiers left as many had been evacuated to other places, maybe to the mainland, and probably through their own efforts once they knew the war was over. This duty proved to be very interesting because the islands were jungles with many mountains and caves and required a lot of time for a thorough cleanup. Given the scope of such a large task and several islands to cover, we spent much time aboard ship going here and there.

Hurricanes are common in that part of the world, and we were caught in one once while in transit from one island to another. It was a horrible experience and it lasted forever, or so it seemed. I believe that there are not many more experiences that are as serious and dangerous as being aboard a ship during such a storm. The ship just bounced around like a cork in a bottle. Nothing on the decks stayed tied down; trucks, oil drums, whatever was on board got dislodged. And, on top of that, the troops were all getting sick and there were not enough restrooms to accommodate us all, so one had to just let it happen. Talk about a bad situation. This was the worst! The biggest danger resulted from so many ships being alongside one another and the potential for collision.

The ship that I was on was an LST. These were fantastic ships because they could carry a tremendous load. However, they were designed with a flat-bottomed hull, so it seemed they just floated on top of the water, and with every wave action, the ship climbed upward and then came down on its flat bottom as the wave crested, raising hell with everything on and everybody inside of the ship. I bet that we were in that hurricane for a day and a night in total, or it could have been a million days. Finally we were able to anchor close to an island so that we could recover from our ordeal. Upon recovering, we had to commence again with our mission and off we went by landing craft to another island.

Okinawa was and had been the main United States objective to invade. Fortunately for us, several of Okinawa's outlying islands were not invaded nor had experienced fighting; consequently, everything we observed was as it had been before the war. Those incidental islands that were occupied by Japanese troops were typically manned by small contingents of soldiers or navy personnel, or in a few cases many personnel, who had weapons and equipment to defend themselves. One small island such as this that we inspected was a little naval base with maybe fifteen to twenty torpedo speedboats. Once we secured this island, we then had more time to closely inspect these craft and determined that they were suicide watercraft equipped with a torpedolike bomb at the bow. Their purpose was to attack an American naval ship and sink or severely damage it upon collision. These craft were approximately twenty feet long and had two souped-up Chevrolet engines to go as fast as they could. Some of the most adventuresome guys were able to get some of these boats started and would have played with them had they not been quickly stopped by superiors. I don't know if there is a record of any of these lethal boats ever being used in defense of Japan and/or surrounding islands.

On some of these isolated islands we discovered naval and army personnel who could have put up a fight should they have chosen to do so. Consequently, we had to be forceful in getting them assembled, and gathering up their equipment to dump into the ocean. Some of these captives were not too anxious to be taken as prisoners, but with some loud hollering and rifle butting, they got the message. After all the equipment was disposed of, these captives were ushered to their barracks and left there to fend for themselves, to be eventually transported back to Japan. How that was accomplished was not known to us nor was it our immediate responsibility.

At one particular island that had experienced some war activity, the Japanese navy and army personnel that we confronted were anxious to be friendly. We stayed for a few days on this island due to the large amount of equipment that had to be gathered and destroyed. This island might have been Ie Shima, a larger island where Ernie Pyle—a great American war correspondent who was very popular with American servicemen—was killed. Well, as men are sometimes more apt to get friendlier with time, even with the enemy, one thing led to another and we discovered we had things to trade with these captives. They wanted cigarettes, chocolate candy, and C rations. These Japanese men really wanted this stuff, so the bartering got started. First sake for cigarettes, then candy and other things for more sake, and then after we all had a glow on, the women were next. Their sake was provided in two-foot-high bottles with a neck of eight inches and volume of one-half gallon. Some of our soldiers bartered for what all of us believed at the time to be Japanese comfort women, and these females were consensually willing, so it became a big party. A few of the guys got their asses hauled in or otherwise screwed in the deal (no pun intended). I bartered for the Japanese flag that my youngest son Tony currently possesses; it came from a Japanese soldier who wanted cigarettes.

After a while everything settled down again and we were back to doing our job. Some of us had had a little too much sake than was good for us, and after a good hangover we once again had order. De-arming this island was a huge job because there were a lot of service personnel stationed here and everything had to be secured and well guarded. These particular Japanese troops were some of the reserve troops to be used whenever they were needed, but after their ships were sunk, they were just there with no place to go except for the hills. Some of them did just that, but we got them all back—not an easy chore.

Close to Okinawa there were many atolls or small, coral-reefed islands, which were defended by somebody, usually very few Japanese. We had to secure all of these smaller areas, which only required a smaller-sized platoon group: thirty to forty of us to go ashore on a landing craft and accomplish the task. In that area of the Pacific storms came up at the drop of a hat and changed calm seas to treacherous oceans. During one of our landings to secure an atoll, a smaller contingent of our troops, about twenty-five men, were put ashore and expected to complete their job. This was a smaller atoll, maybe a mile by half a mile, and it had heavy, jungle-like terrain. This shore party was commanded by Moseley and me, both sergeants at that time. As our smaller group came ashore, we just expected not to meet any defense, which was a good thing for us, as there was a small contingent of Japanese naval personnel, lightly armed and well established in their camp. By this time most Japanese military had gotten the message of their country's surrender, and these navy personnel understood this, so our landing on this atoll turned out just fine, as did our securing this spec of land.

Once our objective was secured, we headed back to our landing craft. After about an hour's hike, we arrived at the point of pickup, but the craft assigned to do so wasn't there. The sea had become very rough and those piloting the craft most likely did not want to get smashed into the rocks along the shoreline, so we scattered out to try and find a more likely pickup site. Moseley and I and a few other men proceeded to look together. The LST, which was dispatching the landing craft, was a long way from the atoll, but eventually we were able to see the craft on its way as it was being tossed about by the rough seas. After some time we could see that the landing craft was making its way toward a group of our men, which was located about a quarter of a mile down the beach from our position. This pickup turned out to be dangerous and rough as the weather did not give us a break. And since the sea was so rough, Moseley and I could not walk close to the shoreline along the rocks as the crashing waves could beat you to death or knock you off your feet and suck you into the water. We both were in full equipment, about fifty pounds of gear, full pack, ammunition, and rifle, making it more difficult to fight the elements as we attempted to make our way down the beach.

By the time Moseley and I arrived at the pickup point, all hell broke loose and the storm became even more intense. He and I and one other soldier were still on the shore. The landing craft had to pull away from the shore and make another try; it was touch-and-go and we three were sweating it out. Believe it or not, it took us about three hours to successfully complete the pickup. Boy, we were beat! All of the men were finally headed for the LST we called home. Whew! That was too close to being a very bad situation. But we left the atoll knowing our job was completed and secured.

Once on board the captain announced over the PA system that our LST would be heading back to Okinawa, still a long way off. He warned us that given the intensity of the storm, we would not get there any time soon as there was another hurricane coming toward us, so we needed to buckle down everything. There were about six hundred personnel with equipment, trucks, guns, ammunition, oil, gas drums, everything necessary to assist us in our mission. Our convoy was made up of a small group of destroyer escorts, small but fast, and they would sail with our much slower three or four LSTs. Well, with any luck we would reach Okinawa eventually. This was about the middle of November 1945. The hurricane continued to get more intense, and our trip back to home base was not to be an easy one. We got hit by the "mother" of all hurricanes for about two or three days. It was just pure hell: seasickness; confusion; equipment, which was previously secured, coming loose; fifty-gallon drums full of oil and gas tumbling about; trucks and artillery guns that were once tied down now tossed around; waves that buried the ship; and people just staying wrapped around something in order to have a sense of security—and so it went. In fact, we lost a man overboard who was attempting to lash down equipment. Finally, Okinawa, our home port, was in sight.

Our first priority upon arrival was to get ashore, knowing that it would not be an easy task. It was still storming when we finally got ashore, so we looked for a place to get out of the weather. Some of us found caves that had been burial places for the people who had lived there for years and years. The living had placed the bones of the deceased in huge jugs and stacked them in these burial caves. Well, we imagined the dead couldn't be hurt too much by the storm, so we threw the jugs out, bones and all, and we climbed inside the place. It didn't smell very pleasant but we were out of the storm. It was quite an experience, but in life you sometimes have to do what you have to do.

After the storm had passed and things returned to a somewhat normal routine, we were placed into a huge camp, hundreds of tents and a lot of kitchens to feed the troops. This was going to be our separation camp. From here one got to board ship and be sent home. For us the war was over and we had done what was asked of us. It wasn't much but we had seen the other part of the world where a terrible war had really happened and there had been fighting that cost the Americans and the Japanese many lives and hardships. And though we did not participate in nor contribute to those terrible episodes, we had been prepared to do so and we were alive, thank God!

Overseas Duty Calls Me

This photo was taken on Okinawa after the invasion began. What my father describes in his writings is indicative of numerous ships, personnel, and materiel in his convoy, and others, that would have had a similar visual impact on the eye of the observer as ships beach and unload men, equipment and supplies necessary for the previously anticipated invasion of the large island of Japan. Military public domain photo.

Aerial view of the devastation of Naha. United States Marine Corp public domain photo, number HD-SN-99-02994.

Torpedo speedboats discovered and destroyed by my father's battery of army personnel. Photo from my father's service album.

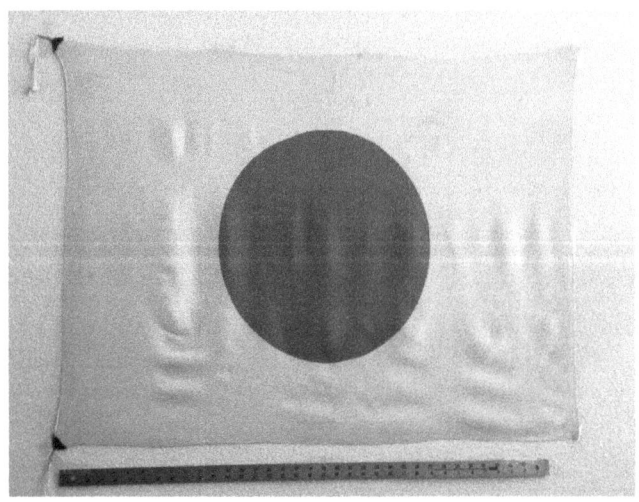

The Japanese flag my father bartered for with a surrendered Japanese soldier wanting cigarettes. Note the metal yardstick below the flag to provide a size frame of reference to reader. Flag is red sun on aged white background. Photo taken by my wife, Patty.

PART EIGHT

DECEMBER 1945–1952

A Homecoming to Remember;
My Civilian Life Begins

Richard, Janet, and new daughter, Sherry Lynn, 706 Dearborn Street. What a merry and special Christmas it was for my young and loving parents and family. Mom's photo album.

CHAPTER EIGHTEEN

Life was easy in the separation camp while we waited to return home. Nothing was demanded of us other than to wait for our time to go aboard ship when our turn came. To occupy ourselves while we waited for our turn to board a ship, we soldiers went for walks or did anything that would add interest or excitement to our loafing time. Some of us played baseball, read, went into the hills to observe where the fighting had been deadly, or toured damaged Japanese cities or war equipment. Some of us even returned to revisit dead Japanese soldiers still lying out in the rugged terrain, caves, or tunnels. When we did visit the hills, we had to have our rifles just in case of trouble with isolated pockets of soldiers who might not have gotten the message or refused to surrender. Others at camp enjoyed playing cards as there was a lot of gambling and serious money being won and lost.

Thanksgiving was coming upon us as November came to a close and the army did its best to make things festive with a traditional meal, including some beer and a little whiskey. Life did not change much from day to day during early December, though we were alerted that we would be getting ready to soon leave Okinawa for the States. The system for discharge from the army was based upon the need to have ninety-five points in order to be sent home, and these points did not come easy. One received so many points for the amount of time spent in the service and points for being overseas. By that time most of us in my unit had quite a few points accumulated. I almost had five years of service time, and of that, six months was spent overseas. I was well covered!

Christmas was around the corner and on about December 6, 1945, we were finally told to prepare to board ship. It took us about four days to finish boarding and men had to really move to do that. Surprisingly, all our equipment was left there, so it was not an encumbrance to our loading process. On December 10, we finally sailed from Okinawa, six thousand miles away from Seattle. Life aboard ship was exciting because every day the authorities told us how far we had gone each day, and this time the trip was much faster as we did not have to zigzag but went full steam ahead.

Our transport, the USS *Mellette APA-156*, was very comfortable; it had been a warship and had participated in both Iwo Jima's and Okinawa's invasions, but now played the role of a troop carrier bringing us all home.[8] The best of everything that the army could cook was served at every meal. Our time was our own though there were only so many things one could do to pass the day: sleep, gamble, read, look at the ocean views. Of course, we were all counting the days as Christmas fast approached in 1945. I was now twenty-three years old, and even at that age I was concerned about my responsibilities of coming home to a bigger family. At that time I did not know what our new baby was, boy or girl, and I didn't much care. I just knew I would love coming home.

The trip home was much shorter than when we went overseas. I believe that getting us home before Christmas was very important

---

8   Ibid. USS Mellette.

My Civilian Life Begins

to the captain of the ship. And fortunately, life aboard ship was not that bad. By this time most of us had gotten our "sea legs" and having been through hurricanes, the trip was a piece of cake, especially since we were all headed for home. Thirteen days later on December 23, 1945, we arrived in Seattle to a band playing on the landing dock along with dancing girls. Of course, home to a lot of the soldiers on board was still a long way away for those from New York, Michigan, Texas, Indiana, and other faraway states, but for me, I was now home!

Upon our arrival we had to be trucked to Fort Lewis south of Tacoma in order to report and check in as required. All troops were given passes for the Christmas holidays so that those soldiers wanting to go home could do so as long as they lived close enough. Soldiers going to Seattle from Fort Lewis were bussed to a central downtown location. Once I arrived there, I took a taxi to 706 Dearborn near downtown Seattle. Talk about my heart pounding! With my duffel bag in hand, I knocked on the door of the old storefront on December 25, 1945, Christmas Day. Janet answered the door, and when she saw me, she was so happy. She knew I was coming home but not exactly when that would be. I was so happy to see her and we hugged and squeezed each other. What a moment to be etched in my memory forever! I could see inside the store, which now served as the family's home, the rather large living room, and I noticed that the dinner table was all set and the meal was being served. All the family was there sitting down to eat, including Grandpa, Janet's brothers Charles, Jack, and Cal, sister Beverly, and my son, Dick Jr., in a high chair. When they saw me, they all screamed, "Dick is home, Dick is home," such happiness and excitement, so I had to hug everybody. Dick Jr., who was about two and a half at the time, was so shy that he had to hide his face. Grandpa took one look at me and said that I needed some meat on my bones and that we would certainly work on that. I sure knew what that meant: fantastic home-cooked meals and lots of them.

After I had hugged everyone and before I sat down, Janet said she had a surprise for me. I knew that we had a new baby, but I did not know if it was a boy or a girl. She took my hand, and as we headed for the area that served as our bedroom, I saw a crib and in it was our new daughter, Sherry Lynn. She was so sweet and fast asleep, but I wished she would wake up and even cry. What a beautiful baby! I knew then that whatever life had in store for us, this was a special moment and nothing that ever happens in life would ever erase that time. If one could only relive those special moments again for a minute or an hour, it would be so beautiful! God, we were so happy and excited, but we knew that dinner was on the table and the others were waiting for us to start eating. The family made room for me at the table, and everyone was so full of questions and all were asking them at the same time. Grandpa had made a beautiful turkey dinner with that marvelous dressing he used to make, and lots of gravy and potatoes, sweet yams, and all the trimmings.

It was so good to be home and the army had allowed us to stay there through Christmas until early January 1946. It was such a treat having all the family together and my sweet wife and two beautiful children. I can't recall that anything much happened, but we all had a wonderful time as a family. I was so skinny. I remember one of the family took a photograph at the front door of Janet, Sherry Lynn, and me in my army uniform that looked a couple of sizes too large, but I didn't care. All I knew was that I was home and that everything would be all right. The holidays were fantastic.

And even though we had very little money, we were not destitute and managed to eat well and enjoyed each other's company. All were happy just to spend time doing what other families were doing: celebrating homecomings, the end of the war, Christmas and the New Year, and my soon-to-be civilian status. The time at home went fast but it was a beautiful several days.

The friends from my unit, Cooper and Moseley, also had family in the Seattle area, and we called each other to keep in touch so when the time came we could go back to Fort Lewis together. Having to go back to Fort Lewis was not bad because I knew that soon I would be home to stay for good, and when my friends and I finally reported back, I stayed at the fort for only about three days. Those of us being discharged were reminded during a formal separation orientation that we were now going to be civilians soon, and were given instructions about where to get help if we needed it during our transition. Perhaps most importantly, we were informed of benefits that as civilians all veterans would have available through the GI Bill for advancing one's education and for financing the purchase of a personal residence. Our federal government was most generous with these programs. We then received our final papers and medals we had coming, including good conduct, overseas duty, and a small insignia that was called the ruptured duck, a little yellow eagle to sew on our uniforms to show we were honorably discharged and had served our country. Finally we were given money to pay our trip fares back home. Since they gave me enough money to return to Arizona, and I now lived in Seattle, I had some extra cash along with my final paycheck. That money was needed to see my family through until I could find steady employment.

Cooper and I made a serious promise to one another that we

would keep in touch; his family lived north of Seattle in Stanwood. Moseley, his wife, Lucille and their baby lived in Seattle so Janet and I also kept in touch with them. So by the tenth of January, 1946, I was finally mustered out of the army and on my way home that day for always!

The USS Mellette APA-156 provided the ride home to my father and all of his buddies and many other personnel eligible to return to the States in December 1945. The ride home was a piece of cake compared to the trip over; no zigzagging required. Public domain photo courtesy of NavSource.org.

CHAPTER NINETEEN

In those days for soldiers coming home, the most important thought in a man's mind was to get a permanent job from which you could eventually retire while providing for yourself and your family during your working years. Had I had a high school education, I would have liked to have gone on to college, but at the time my biggest concern was to support my new family and this required that I find permanent work and a steady income. I do not have regrets that I did not take advantage of the GI educational benefits because my family was my main responsibility, and this was my priority. I was most conscious about this need for security as I had never had a home or permanence, but now I was going to work to create these for my growing family.

Cooper and I talked about looking for work as he was also able to settle down in Seattle if needed. He and I decided that some kind of a civil service job would be the most promising for being stable and there were all kinds of jobs available, mostly manual labor jobs. Though I was willing to learn, in my mind I did not have any professional skills, so for the immediate future I decided to seek out a labor job. At that time after war's end there were lots of men looking for work, so the first place we went to was the Seattle

Engineering Department located just about two blocks from 706 Dearborn Street where I lived. Cooper and I talked with a supervisor, a Mr. Nelson, who informed us that they had jobs available for all the returning soldiers. He thanked us for our service to our country and welcomed us to the Engineering Department. He told us that the jobs didn't pay much but the work was ours as long as we wanted it, that it would be a lot different from what we were used to in the military, that promotions were quick, and that all one had to do was display some heart and commitment to the job. Cooper and I started as laborers and were paid $150 a month, so we were set. I believed at the time that for me a laborer's job was OK, but I felt Cooper deserved better as he was older than I and more educated.

The next significant lifestyle concern for returning soldiers at that time was housing for themselves and their families. Cooper and I discussed our options and realized that there wasn't much readily available in Seattle, so we had better start looking. He had a car and I didn't, so we used his vehicle to go house hunting for our respective families. Both he and I had heard about Renton Highlands, a war housing project for defense workers, that happened to have some units available for thirty dollars a month, plus all the coal you needed for cooking and heating. Janet and I and Cooper and his wife, Dorothy, agreed that it was a start, so both of us couples moved maybe three or four weeks after we started our jobs at the Engineering Department. Cooper was tired of commuting from Stanwood to Seattle, and I was ready to set up housekeeping in our own place with my wife and family. Moving was no big deal as Janet and I didn't have much furniture, though we did manage to come up with a few things. Grandpa and the kids were able to get different housing, I believe located in Yesler

Terrace, through the Seattle Housing Authority; the rent there did not cost him much and would be more comfortable than the old store location.

So Janet and I moved to Renton Highlands to housing that was adequate and provided us with all the rooms that we needed; certainly more than what we had been used to. More importantly, we had our privacy and it taught us about living in a house that was only for our small family. However, we did miss Grandpa and all of Janet's brothers and sisters and their activity. Janet did all the cooking and she did such a terrific job as she had learned well from her father. I didn't know anything about cooking, but I helped with the housework and babies. We lived near the Coopers, so they were our main friends. Our next-door neighbors, Frank and Ida Bruni, were from New York and very nice folks. They cooked really good Italian meals.

The Seattle Engineering Department Charles Street Shop location where Dad and Cooper began civilian employment. This building was replaced in 1950 with a new facility of completely different design and appearance. Photo courtesy of the Seattle Municipal Archives depicting the testing of a new hose nozzle. Photo ID number 41026.

Renton Highlands Projects. This Renton Highlands photo was most likely taken in the mid-1950s. However, it seems reasonable that the physical appearance of the buildings from the immediate postwar years would not have changed that much from when my parents moved in during 1946. Photo courtesy of Renton Housing Authority.

CHAPTER TWENTY

Our lives soon became quite normal and routine; though we still did not have many possessions, we got along just fine. Most of the families living in the area were comprised of young veterans struggling to make ends meet and all starting out their lives on the same footing. Our friendship with the Coopers continued to grow; they were raising a family like we were. They might have been used to a little better life as they both had come from more established backgrounds, but they did just fine and our lives were not that different. I was a good family man and Janet was the supreme woman of the house. She was a wonderful wife, mother, companion, and friend.

Time continued swiftly by and things got settled at our jobs with the city. Cooper and I had essentially the same job as most of the other men who had started when we did. He and I were both common laborers using brooms, shovels, and edge-trimming tools; making dirt and grass piles; and then shoveling the stuff onto a dump truck. It took a full day to fill up the truck, but it was a job and very secure I would say. We got to know well the streets of Seattle because we cleaned them all up and down Beacon Hill, Seattle Central District, Magnolia, Capitol Hill, you name it!

However, one day during our daily commute to our workplace in Seattle, Cooper and I finally decided that there had to be a better way to make a living. After four or five months of cleaning up streets, we both agreed to stick it out though as we went about sizing up prospects for employment change. At that time working for the City, we each made about seven dollars per day.

I also determined that I really needed a car as I had been relying on Cooper's to get to and from work and Janet and I required our own means of travel. It just so happened that the truck driver with whom I worked, Bert Salvino, found out I needed an automobile, so he informed me that he wanted to sell his car. It was a 1937 Chevrolet coupe. I had noticed the vehicle in the employee parking lot as it was nice looking: a green, two-door coupe. I asked him how much money he wanted and he told me $200. So we talked about it and for some reason I can't remember, I gave him $250. Man, that was a beautiful, clean automobile, so now my family had a car. Big time! Now Cooper and I could take turns driving to work each day, which made it a little easier on us both.

Time is passing and it is now about June 1946. On one occasion, while Cooper and I were working our usual job, we were told to go to Builders' Brick Company on Airport Way and Spokane Street to pick up some drainage tile for the sewer workers. Now that job was a hell of a lot worse than the job I already had, as working all day in the sewers was not anything I wanted to do permanently. Anyway, Cooper and I picked up the tiles, and while we were there, I asked the boss at Builders' Brick, Tay Cooper, a veteran, if they had any jobs and how much they paid. He said a dollar twenty an hour and yes they did have some jobs available. Well, I thought about it and it did seem to me to be a little better job than what I was currently doing. And I would no longer be out on the streets with everybody looking at me thinking that they had a better job than me. I talked to my friend Cooper about it, and he said he'd been looking around too but had not decided yet on making a move, but he was tired of sweeping streets. We both thought we could do better. We continued working at the Engineering Department, and I discussed with Janet about making the job switch. She thought that maybe it would be better if I thought there would be a little more money. By June 1946 I had decided that working at the brickyard might not be too bad. Cooper in the meantime decided that he would move his family back to Stanwood because they could live with his wife's parents and he had a brother-in-law who might help him get a job at Standard Oil, so that's what we each respectively did.

The green 1937 Chevrolet coupe that was both of my parents' first car. Additional photos taken of my parents and friends, along with the above one, affirmed that they were site seeing and the Chevy had not broken down, at least not at that time. Photo from family album.

CHAPTER TWENTY-ONE

Well, I went to work at Builders' Brick and started all anew again, and I felt that I was improving my financial status. I got a job as a wheeler, which meant that I used a wheelbarrow to cart bricks just out of the drying kiln to where they were temporarily stacked and cooled. It really was a very hot, dirty, and heavy job as one hundred bricks weighing about five pounds apiece made for a big five-hundred-pound load. It sounds more difficult than it really was as the wheelbarrow had a balloon tire and was made to balance easily. The front tire actually carried the weight once you got the feel of how to do it. It took me a little while and I dumped a few loads, but then I got the hang of it and it came easy.

After I had been working at the brickyard a couple of weeks, I had met all the guys employed there. Some of these people had worked there for years, mostly Swedes and Italians, all with humpbacks, fifty to sixty years old. As I was the only young guy working there, they would all tell me that I was the same age as they were when they had started working for Builders' Brick, and they had been too dumb to do anything else. They warned me that continuing to work here would make an old man out of me before

My Civilian Life Begins

my time, and besides, men who had fought the war deserved better than this. I was still commuting from Renton, and the job at the brickyard got easier because I toughened up and was in great physical condition as a result. I did not drink or smoke and Janet's cooking was always good, so I felt in A1 shape, and home life was very content with my sweet, little family.

After I had worked at the brickyard a month or so, the foreman asked me where I lived, so I told him in Renton. He responded that there was another war housing project of very nice duplexes located at High Point in the West Seattle area, and that I would be a lot closer to work. The foreman had a cousin who lived there and liked it quite well. So I soon checked it out and showed it to Janet. High Point at that time was a very nice area, which really impressed us, and Janet thought that it would be great to be closer to my work. She also had friends living near there that she could now visit more conveniently. We applied to live there, but at the time there was a waiting list of four or five months due to the many veterans being placed with their young families. So once we could gain admission, we would fit right in. This was about July of 1946.

The thought of eventually going to work for the City of Seattle kept stirring my interest. Since Builders' Brick Company was only about six blocks from Seattle City Light shops located at 4th and Spokane Street, one day after work I drove over to ask one of the City Light workers how one could get a job there. He informed me about what I needed to do in order to be considered for employment. So I decided to continue my job at the brickyard while I was seeking employment at Seattle City Light through the civil service system. I told them that I had worked for the Seattle Engineering Department but that I wanted to work for City Light. One day the civil service folks called me about a laborer's exam coming up and informed me that if I was interested, I should report to civil service and be ready to take a hard, physical exam that would include heavy labor work. I did take the exam and though it was hard, it was all heavy lifting, pulling and moving items, plus oral and written tests. I passed the whole thing. Heck, I was in such good shape from working in the brickyard! Several of the men did not pass the exam, so I got on the list. Unfortunately, because I lived outside of the city limits, they couldn't hire me until I moved into the city or all the applicants in the city were first hired.

About the end of September 1946, we received a call from the High Point Housing Project informing Janet and me that there was a unit available if we still wanted it. We sure did want it! So we made plans to move, and by this time we had accumulated some furniture: a couch, chairs, and such. She and I went to 3402 Lanham Way to see the unit we would occupy and saw that it was very tidy and clean, with two bedrooms, a stove and refrigerator, gleaming hardwood floors and countertops, plenty of kitchen cabinets, a large living room and dining area, and a nice bathroom, and it was newly painted inside and out. The unit also had a partial basement and a coal furnace. We would have all the space in the world. It was a dream come true. Wow! Janet and I were so happy.

As we were moving from Renton, the mailman came and I had received a letter from civil service asking when could I report to work for the Seattle City Light Department. I had a job that I wanted! Talk about two of the happiest people in the world; it all fell together for us. Of course, I called the civil service office first thing Monday, the end of September 1946, and they asked me to report to the Seattle City Light office located at 3rd and Madison. I was to speak with a Mr. Hoffman, whose office was on the third floor. He was a big boss; though not yet a superintendent of City

Light, he would later become that man. When I went to see him, he welcomed me to the department and said they were most happy to be hiring veterans, and that I was one of many being hired at that time by City Light. I was told to report to the appliance repair office in the basement of the City Light Building on October 6, 1946.

I still had the job at the brickyard for another four or five days. I never wished as I did then that time would hurry and go by fast so that I could start my new employment working in a nice, clean, inside job. When it came time to leave the brickyard, I thanked all the guys for all that I had learned from them and said that I had enjoyed being part of the team. They told me that I was making a good move and they had been happy to have a hard worker on the crew and then wished me well.

A new job and better pay for Richard and his family. Assessor's Office 1944 photograph of Builders' Brick facility. This building was torn down in 1965. Photo courtesy of Puget Sound Regional Archives, Washington State.

My Civilian Life Begins

The new Seattle City Light office building completed in 1936, Third and Madison. This location was where my father initially worked upon being hired by Seattle City Light. Note that later in Chapter 23 there is a humorous story concerning the alley behind this building and my father's first day on the job in the electrical appliance service shops. Photo courtesy of the Seattle Municipal Archives; item number 10259.

CHAPTER TWENTY-TWO

On October 6, 1946, I reported to the City Light appliance service shops and met John Delong, the supervisor, in addition to several other men, mostly young veterans recently hired like me. There were also some of the older men who had worked there several years. I was assigned to the repair shop working for two gentleman named Tony Rouse and Jim Gross, both old-timers. They showed me around the shop and where to find things necessary to do the job, and were very kind and nice to me. My first job there was winding hot plate and oven elements on the winding machine. Wow! I was learning electrical work. The workers here were a different class—journeyman electricians with years of knowledge. Most of the new guys had been in the navy, really nice men as I think of them now, most of whom have passed on. What a tremendous experience I was having during my starting days at Seattle City Light.

Sometimes if there was a job that somebody needed help with in the field, I got to go with them, and these guys knew that I was just a laborer starting, so they taught me a lot about the job. John Erickson, Sy Simore, and Ole Olson, the guys that needed help most often because they did really heavy work with stoves and water heaters, all would take time to teach me. They suggested that I get some basic electrical books and they would then test me on what I had learned. These three were fantastic people, and when they had spare time, they would take me aside and instruct me as to what they were doing. A fourth person, Jonesy, the oven man, always took me with him when he had some heavy work to do, mostly in kitchens and restaurants.

Sometime around February 1947, Seattle City Light was in the process of negotiating to purchase the Puget Power Company in Seattle, as it was a competing business within the city. However, a lot of changes were being made even before the transition was finalized, all of which would benefit Seattle City Light. In April 1947, I had been with City Light for about five months, and Janet told me that our little family was going to get bigger as she was pregnant again. She told me that the baby would probably arrive sometime in late November or early December. I could not have been happier because everything looked great for us as my job was secure and I could work toward further opportunities for advancement. So our little family would certainly get my best because they were my treasure.

City Light was sure a good opportunity for our family and I was very happy with my job, so all of my work reflected my good attitude. Consequently, my supervisors appreciated that fact. My job of making range cables became quite a large project because there were thousands of houses that needed to be changed to the City Light system. The basement where I worked was loaded with all kinds of electrical materials, so my job looked like a never-ending one, which was OK with me.

The months went by and on December 3, 1947, our family

grew by one. Tony was born. Janet had a very difficult time with him because his was a breach birth and Janet had so many false alarms, which stressed us both to no end. Finally while in labor for some time, Janet's doctor decided that she had to have a caesarian because the baby was ready to be born and could not be delivered. It was a most emotional and painful time for both of us, mainly for Janet. The doctors decided to give a normal delivery one last chance and Janet finally delivered. It was a most happy day for us both because mother and baby were fine and Dad also survived. The people at West Seattle Hospital were so good to us during this difficult time, and we were so grateful to them. Janet stayed in the hospital about four days, which was OK because I was in charge at home as the chief cook and bottle washer; taking care of the kids was perfect for me. I don't really know how I happened to get the time off, maybe vacation. When Janet came home with the baby, it was a real happy house, as always. Our home was always a most happy place as my wife somehow made everything OK and I tried my best to be a good husband and father. Dick Jr. and Sherry Lynn both knew that they now had a new baby brother.

My Civilian Life Begins

My mother's triumphant return home from giving birth to me nestled on her lap, along with my brother Richard Jr., in the middle, with sister Sherry Lynn on Dad's lap. This photo was taken at the Lanham duplex located within the High Point Housing Project. Photo from family album.

CHAPTER TWENTY-THREE

At the City Light Third and Madison building I was still doing my job of making cables to retrofit customers' ranges. I must have done that job for about a year as well as help the appliance people when they needed it, mostly heavy lifting or moving items requiring two people. However, I was always learning the electrical details of things. I bought some basic electrical books and the guys helped me when I needed it. The City Light electricians I helped informed me of a school, Central School I believe, located about six blocks from the City Light building, that had night classes on electricity, so I enrolled using the GI Bill benefits available to veterans. This meant that I would be going to night classes, and Janet thought that it would be good because I would make more money. If I took a helpers' exam and got promoted, I could make as much as $12.50 a day, which at that time was all the money in the world.

City Light had exams frequently for lineman helpers, so I started school at night from 6:00 to 9:00 p.m., which made for a long day, but in the end I felt it would pay off. Janet was very supportive so we were both happy with the decision. For quite a while I did laborers' work, but I was learning more and more about electricity and getting more comfortable with the job that I was doing. After having spent time in the appliance division, I transferred to the underground section, still as a laborer. This underground work was more dangerous, the workers more intense and demanding as they worked with higher voltages and were paid more money for doing so.

My most memorable workday at City Light was my first day in the underground network. I was to work with a wireman helper as my boss. His name was Carl Presho. He was an overseer of the work that I was to be doing, and he might as well have been Jesus Christ because I really respected him. He told me our job was going to be in the alley right behind the City Light building off of Madison, and would entail digging a ditch about forty feet long and about one foot deep. So he took me to a supply room and I drew out the necessary tools, including a pry bar, shovel, a wheelbarrow, and a broom to keep the alley clean. I also obtained some barriers to blockade the alley from vehicle and foot traffic. Well, he marked where the ditch was supposed to be and he just proceeded to look like a boss. The alley was paved with bricks and the work went sort of slow, but because all the big supervisors and management personnel went in and out of the basement by way of the alley, we had to keep active and look alive.

Carl and I really started our job seriously about 8:20 a.m. and so the work began with removing the brick first and exposing where the ditch was to be dug. About 9:00 a.m. Carl said we were going to take a break, so I thought to myself, "Wow! A break, we just got started." So I said to Carl, "OK, I have an apple and some hot coffee in my lunch box. I'll get that." "No, no," he said, "put up the barricade and we'll walk down to Jerry's about two blocks down this alley." When we got to Jerry's, I found out that it was a cocktail bar and sandwich place. I was worried because I only had about $1.25 with me for bus fare and a few extra pennies. When we got in to sit down, everybody knew Carl Presho and they all greeted him by name. He greeted the bartender and the waitresses, and we sat at the bar and I ordered a cup of coffee. Carl said, "No, no, we are going to have a beer." Well, he was the boss and he told the bartender that he had a new City Light worker here and that he was going to treat me to a real break. So I had a glass of beer at 9:00 a.m. and he had two!

We got back to the job site, and I continued to work on removing the bricks and putting dirt in the wheelbarrow and he continued to be boss. About ten thirty he said we needed another break. Carl and I had been back from the first break about an hour, so I put my tools aside and barricaded the ditch and we were off to Jerry's. We got there and inside were some different folks this time. They all said hi to Carl. "How's City Light? Working hard?" Carl said, "No, today I have a new worker with me and his name is Dick, and we both need a break." So he said how do's to the bartender and ordered two beers. I was thinking, "Boy, this is sure different than the brickyard!" At 11:00 a.m. we left; I had one beer, Carl had two. I got back to my work and I was working hard, so I didn't feel the two beers; Carl had had four. He said, "Dick you don't have to work as hard as you are working. They don't expect you to kill yourself, just keep moving. They don't expect me to work too hard because I am the boss."

At about eleven forty-five Carl said, "Button up the work area and then we'll go to lunch." I said to Carl that I brought my lunch so I would just go into the bullpen and eat. He said, "No, no, you come and we'll go to Jerry's and have lunch. They have pretty good soup and sandwiches." So, well, I didn't want to get on his bad side the first day on the job, so I followed Carl to Jerry's. We had an hour for lunch, so it was a long one. While I was eating my sandwich, he continued to drink but this time it was whiskey with a chaser of beer. Finally the lunch hour was over and I thought, "Thank God." Carl yawned and stretched and then he said, "I think we should have one for the road." I said thanks but I was full. "No, no," he said, "bartender give me a water-back and give my friend another beer." I thought, "Whew!" Well, we had our drinks and by this time it was after one o'clock. So we sauntered back up to the job and I continued my work.

About two o'clock Carl said he thought it had been a long day so we should have another break, so off we went to Jerry's. He had two beers, I had one. I don't believe that he had had a bite of solid food all day; he just drank. We got back to the job about two thirty and at three thirty we had to visit Jerry's again. Carl had the usual two beers and one for me. We got back around four o'clock and I had to put the tools away, so I went to the bullpen to wash up before going home. By this time when I got on the bus to go home, I was feeling no pain and thinking, "What the hell am I going to tell my wife about why I'm feeling so loose?" Well, the ditch job only lasted one day because it was decided that a bigger crew with a backhoe and dump truck were needed to do the job quickly, as it had somehow become an emergency to get it done. Thank God it was over!

CHAPTER TWENTY-FOUR

Having survived my one day with Carl Presho, my next assignment was to work in the tool room where the tools were all stored. Some of these items I had never seen before, and they comprised all the electrical tools and parts for splicing cables. At the time City Light only used lead cables, so I had a lot of learning to do. The foreman, a man named George Sterrett, asked me how I liked working with Peeps, a nice old guy about fifty years old who was the regularly assigned person in charge of the tool room. I thought he was really old but very good and a willing teacher. In hindsight now I know that he was not old at all. In the tool room you had to know the parts that the linemen needed to perform their work so when they put their orders in the night before for work the next day, it had better be right. Peeps was a lot of help to me in learning about filling these orders while familiarizing myself with the many types of tools available.

The cable splicing crews consisted of a cable splicer, a wireman helper, and a maintenance laborer. I wanted to somehow work myself into a splicing crew, and I let it be known around the shop. After I had been there for six months, George came to me

My Civilian Life Begins

and asked me if I would like to be on the splicing crew. He told me that I had been a very good worker in the tool room and that I had learned a lot, and he felt that I was ready. I said yes, indeed I would. He then told me that the change would make me "top man" on this particular crew, that the crew would depend on me to do a good job, and that I would get a little more pay as these crews work some overtime. The top man's role was to essentially provide the more experienced workers down in the electrical vault all of the necessary tools, equipment, or assistance needed so they could complete their tasks. Since this person was aboveground, he was called a "top man."

So Monday morning I was assigned to work with Spence Driver, the cable splicer, one of the most respected workers at City Light. His helper was a nice guy named Jim McKillops. Spence did not fool around, and if there was work to be done, he'd do it, so he kept our crew busy. There were a lot of things that I had to learn to become a good top man, including all the necessary tasks to make a correct splice. And as the laborer on the crew, they depended on me to have things ready when needed in the electrical vault. I was able to learn much more at this particular job because this was heavy electrical work. In 1949 the underground division was the highest-paying electrical job in City Light and offered good opportunities for advancement. Of course, it would take some time, but I had a lot of that, and all I had to do was keep my nose clean, listen, and learn, as everybody was willing to help if one showed any initiative.

I liked the work in the underground division, and the guys liked me because I never fooled around. If there was work to be done, I did it! Most of the crews were a little loose at times, but Spence, my crew boss, was a little too old for fooling around.

Because he knew I enjoyed working and wanted to learn, he liked training me, telling me what a job was all about and the dangers involved. He would take me down into the vault and tell me about the equipment that was there—the transformers, the cables, the protectors, the cut-out switches—how they all worked, and what he expected of me as part of the crew. During those times the promotions came slow and Spence wanted me to learn all that I could because it would help me pass the electrical exams. He stressed quite strongly that the work was dangerous because of the high voltages down in the vault. Spence knew I was going to Central School studying electricity, and he would help me with my studies. He was one fantastic person.

After working with Spence for about two years, I decided I needed to make a little more money. The fireman's helper job I wanted was a slow process because there were not too many of those jobs available. But there were some helper jobs available in the line divisions, though these didn't pay as much as they were not as intricately involved with electricity. Instead, it was a lot of physical work out in the weather. Hard labor for a strong back was the standard for that job. It was a very different type of work—not too demanding of electrical knowledge but still dangerous. This job also paid more money than I was making as a top man on a splicing crew. The workers were also a little more rough-and-tumble in character, way different from the splicing crew personalities. The exam finally came for lineman helper and I passed it, as by this time I knew quite a bit about City Light and the different types of work required throughout the company.

In 1951 I became a lineman helper; my workstation was located at 4th Avenue South and Spokane Street. This was going to be a lot different work, all of it outside, rain or shine, no sitting in the truck for the weather to change. It was also a lot of fun. When one was new at the line division, one started at the lowest job, and if you showed you could work, you were transferred to other more dangerous work. I started in the pole yard where all the line poles were stocked. In this yard there was a large machine that peeled all the bark off of the poles. It was a dirty, noisy, dangerous job and I worked my butt off, but after a time I toughened up and then it was just a job. There were about five lineman helpers and a machine operator who had no mercy for us helpers; we had to earn our $11.50 per day, and he saw to that. I worked there about six months and then went to work on the pole-setting crew.

On this particular crew there were about six helpers, a foreman, a machine operator for the pole-digging machine, and a truck driver named Fats Hamiliton—and boy, was he heavy. We also had a lineman on this crew by the name of Bill Barrens, a young veteran. All of the linemen thought they were next to God, so we had to show Bill respect as his job was to protect us from hot wires as we were placing poles through them. My foreman's name was Panhandle Pete, who had been a lineman for about a hundred years and he looked like it. He was a funny man who teased the hell out of all of us crewmen. On one hand he was missing two fingers, a thumb and forefinger. He would stick his missing thumb up his nose and we would laugh and say, "Pete's picking his nose." He would say, "We're going to set a line of poles today and I don't want anybody to stop to pick their nose. I'll do that." In 1951 we put up poles from Northgate in north Seattle, to a substation that is now close to the downtown civic center. A lot of those poles are still up today.

About summer of 1951 I was transferred to a heavy crew in the line division working for Bob Stinson, a very good foreman and a real worker. There were six linemen and seven helpers. The linemen included all young war veterans full of hell but terrific workers; they worked the hell out of the helpers of which I was one. This type of crew was responsible for all the "heavy" line work and big jobs. On this crew we hung all the high lines on the poles that I had helped to place from Northgate to Seattle. That was a very long job, but we made a lot of extra money due to overtime.

CHAPTER TWENTY-FIVE

By this time, since my family was getting larger and needed another bedroom, Janet and I submitted our request for a three-bedroom unit, wanting to remain in the High Point neighborhood. Our present unit was close to the store and bus, and the kids could walk and play in a traffic-free cul-de-sac. Dick Jr., who was seven, and Sherry Lynn being five, could both walk to school; Tony was only three at the time. Grandpa was still living in Seattle at Yesler Terrace, and Janet's brothers Cal, Charlie, and Jack and sister Bev were all getting older and more independent. Janet was worried about Grandpa being on his own more and more, so she and I imagined that Grandpa could move in with us if we could get a three-bedroom unit.

Finally we got such a unit also located in the West Seattle High Point Housing Project on Cycle Lane, close to our current rental on Lanham Way. We were so excited because it was larger and it had a little bit of a view toward Seattle. Now that we had more room, Dick Jr. had his own bedroom, Sherry Lynn and Tony shared one, and Janet and I had our own too. In time, Grandpa moved in with us and then Dick Jr. shared his room with him. Though we were a little crowded, it was OK as we were comfortable with our nice family and all seemed to be happy. Janet quickly met our attached duplex neighbors, Otis and Margie Neet, who also had two kids at that time. We eventually became real close friends with them and over several years created with our families many wonderful experiences and memories together.

I continued to work in the line division for about two years. My eventual goal was to get back to the underground division, but in order to do that, I had to pass the wireman helpers' exam. I had more experience now with electrical work and I was still going to school taking classes that would prepare me for the wireman helpers' exam. When that exam was offered, I easily passed it as by this time I had learned a lot about what was expected of the job. However, I discovered that line work was not for me, mainly because I didn't like climbing poles. The thing that changed my mind about the work came on me as I climbed a ninety-foot pole located by Northgate. This pole was bare and I had to put some crossarms at the very top of the pole. As I looked down at my feet, my knees were shaking and Bob Stinson, my foreman, noticed right away and asked me to come down. That was enough for me! Since I had passed the wireman helpers' exam, I got my chance to go back to the underground division making $12.50 a day, all the money in the world, or so I thought.

I started to work for Carl Brown, a journeyman, with me as his helper, and Doc Wildman as the top man; we had quite a crew. Carl was a very good teacher and the experience of working with him was fantastic. He was full of stories, as he was a South Park cocksman who lived down at La Cantina Tavern. I was Carl's helper for a long time. Doc Wildman was a real nice person. God, was he strong. He would say to me, "Hit me as hard as you can on my stomach, do it man." I'd wind up and hit him and it was like hitting a wall. He thought that was so funny; then he'd laugh at me because he said he didn't feel a thing.

Sometime in 1953 or early 1954 the employment notice was posted for cable splicer. I had a lot of experience by then with splicing as Carl had taught me everything that I needed to know about the work. So to further prepare for that exam, after work I went at night to Broadway High School on Capitol Hill to take more electrical classes. I needed more education on electrical theory and power transmission. This meant that I was gone a lot of the evening, but Janet had so much to do with three small kids, it wasn't a problem. I also believe that Grandpa lived with us then at Cycle Lane and had lived with us for some time, so Janet had to assist him as well.

The Cycle Lane duplex that would be our family's home until sometime in 1953. In the photo my father is at the driver's side window of the newer 1949 Chevrolet, and in the background my sister Sherry Lynn is on the far right with her backside facing the camera, and at center of the photo Uncle Cal is squatting, with Uncle Jack having his hands on his knees. Photo from family album.

PART NINE

1953-1975

More Good Memories;
I Transition from Blue Collar to White Collar Employment;
My Personal Life Choices of Family Consequence

My father, Richard, in his mid-sixties. This photo is one of four bound in a picture folio given as gifts from Dad in the late 1980s to both my siblings and me.

CHAPTER TWENTY-SIX

Somehow, through all of the family and career life changes, we still managed to have a wonderful, loving life. As a family we did a lot of camping with our neighbors Otis and Margie and their three children. The happiest times of all our lives were the razor clam-digging camping trips to the Washington coast, usually at Copalis Beach north of Ocean Shores. Our families would just do relaxing, fun things with our kids, take walks on the beach, dig clams, build campfires, and steam the clams. Our two families got along so well that we all enjoyed our shared trips together. There were so many of them during the fifties to the Washington and Oregon coasts, San Juan Islands, California, Canada, Idaho, and Montana. Life was so grand. Sometimes you wonder why life has to change, but life is like that.

I remember when we lived at 6210 Cycle Lane our lives were very much in balance and going our way. Around 1952 we bought our first television, a black-and-white one that was quite an addition to our household, because in those days, all the TV programs were quite decent and the whole family could enjoy the programming. We even frequently had many of the neighborhood kids over to watch television as very few families had a TV during those years.

Around that same time, Otis and Margie had purchased a home in the Burien area on First Avenue and 148th Street. But we remained very close and continued to have our fun times together. Janet and I would take the kids over to visit the Neets at their new home and have picnics in their large yard. At the time they used to raise chickens and we would butcher them for BBQs. The kids would gather around Otis and me as we chopped a chicken's head off and the bird would jump high in the air and the kids would scream as the headless chickens always seemed to be chasing the screaming kids. What a zoo that was! All of us sure enjoyed the BBQed chicken; man, what days those were.

Also about this time in the early 1950's, during the afternoons after public school was out, Janet started providing day care for a youngster named Dennis Monroe. He was the stepson of James Harris and son of James's wife, Hazel. I don't recall how Janet got started doing this, but she was paid a little money for doing so and we eventually became good friends with the Harris family. James sold real estate and owned a used car lot in White Center, while his wife, Hazel, had an office job. I had spoken with James occasionally about my need for an automobile, and he just happened to have a four-door 1938 sedan for sale that was well used but could be cheaply purchased. He gave me a deal I couldn't refuse! Anyway, we used this car when camping as it carried all of our gear, though it burned about three quarts of oil just to get to the ocean. This car worried the heck out of my young son Tony. He would stand behind me on the center hump on the floor in back of the front seat and talk into my ear as I drove, saying, "Are we there yet? When will we get there? Will it be dark? How many more miles? Do we have enough gas? Did you check the oil, Dad?" What a wonderful life we had; why couldn't it always be like that? Our future looked very promising and our family was growing and things looked great.

Going to the ocean in those days was a long trip. We had to pass through Tacoma, Washington, using Highway 99, as freeways did not exist then; traffic was always heavy and travel was slow. It is only about 135 miles to where we typically camped, just outside of Copalis Beach. Even so, in those days it took us about six hours travel time. Our families would leave Seattle on Friday night after work. Janet and Margie would pack the cars beforehand, and when it was time to go, they had everything ready. Otis and I would get home from work and we'd be on our way. We would get to Copalis about eleven o'clock at night, then set up the tents, which in the dark sometimes was both hilarious and frustrating, next get something to eat, and then go to bed, looking forward to digging clams the next morning.

In the morning Janet and Margie would prepare breakfast while the kids went out and played. Both families would then eat and all jump in the cars and go to the beach to dig clams. At that time each capable person could take eighteen clams, so we would come back with a couple of buckets full. Otis and I would spend the day cleaning and preparing the clams for either clam chowder or fritters, or steam them whole that evening while we all sat around the campfire. To do this, Otis and I would make a big fire and would burn much wood to generate lots of hot, burning coals. We then placed the cleaned clams in wet paper surrounded by pin-pricked tin foil and buried them for several minutes under the hot coals. Once they were steamed, we would take them out and have a feast. Boy, what a tasty way to eat them! Everyone enjoyed eating those razor clams.

Our families spent many wonderful times at the ocean because we all enjoyed it so much and it was an inexpensive way to vacation and have fun. What a fantastic way to raise our children. I'm sure they treasured those memories as well. Now it would be impossible to do the same as everything has changed. The places where we camped then are no longer accessible, there are more people, more restrictions, and the public seems to be more careless about respecting the environment or the property of others. In our day, we would leave camp for hours and upon our return everything would be as we left it. Not anymore. Now when you leave something unguarded, it seems somebody will trash the place and help themselves to your belongings.

Another great Washington State location that was our haven for vacations and weekend getaways was the county park north of Friday Harbor on San Juan Island. It was a nice-sized, somewhat informal campground with Puget Sound waterfront galore. This park was located away from traffic, not used by too many folks, and had several acres of grass, trees, camping spots, fresh water, and numerous opportunities for the kids to enjoy themselves. Otis would sometimes go saltwater fishing for rock fish or cod, but primarily the adults and kids just enjoyed beautiful leisure times as our families were so compatible together. Patty Kay and Sherry Lynn, our daughters, would go looking for seashells or amuse themselves with their dolls, and Janet and Margie would get their time to relax and enjoy each other's company, and a respite from their family demands.

A secondary purpose traveling to the island was to hunt the many rabbits that at that time inhabited it. Through my employment at City Light I had a friend whose family lived on the island, owning and farming several acres of land. In fact, sometime earlier on, I had been invited by and previously hunted rabbits on the island with this person, along with a couple other City Light employees. So I knew the routine and what to expect. My resident friend always gave Otis and me permission to hunt on their property when we were on vacation there. Otis and I would take along our young sons Jim, Dick Jr., and Tony, each of us armed with a 22-caliber rifle, anticipating the BBQ that would come later in the day; as always we would bag several rabbits. All the boys had attended gun-handling classes, so they were prepared and knew how to be safe. Upon returning from our hunts, the kids would gather around and watch with closed eyes as Otis and I skinned the rabbits and butchered them for the BBQ. Margie and Janet would be busy planning and preparing our dinner, and man, what a meal we would have!

One activity that just the four adults did, Otis, Margie, Janet, and I would actually net rabbits—rather than shoot them—over a few hours very late at night. This was a whole lot of fun and we had many laughs while doing it. My friend who owned the farm had converted an old jalopy with two tractor seats mounted on the running boards on both sides of the vehicle, a portable, high-beam spotlight mounted on the windshield, and two wire cages mounted on the back with lift-up tops to place the captured rabbits. We would drive out into the fields late at night with no lights around, and a person would sit on each tractor seat, one of whom would hold a fifteen-foot pole with an oval-shaped open end having a webbed net strung around it. While driving through a field, one would spot a rabbit and turn the high-beam light on it that would freeze the rabbit motionless. At the same time the person holding the pole nearest the dazed rabbit would reach out and cover it with the net. Once covered, the rabbit would usually try to get away and become entangled in the net. This would allow it to be lifted up in the net, and with a gloved hand grabbing the hind legs, the person would place it in the secure wire boxes at the back of the jalopy. This night technique would enable one to get several rabbits in a short time, and I believe it was typically used when one wanted to get as many rabbits as needed to butcher, flash freeze, and take home for eating. There was no established hunting limit at the time as there were thousands of rabbits on the island, though in later years they were mostly eradicated either through island edict or plague. Not sure.

During these vacation times our families had lives that couldn't be better. And each day when we woke up, we knew that the new day would be just as much fun and satisfying as the day before. All the adults and our kids just loved this place. One particular image comes to mind while we camped at the San Juan County park. Sherry Lynn, Patty Kay, and Johnny Neet, Patty's little brother, who was probably three or four years old at the time, were all watching a skin diver spearfishing off of a small island not too far from shore. They were all very interested in what this skin diver was doing as at the time on TV there was a show starring Lloyd Bridges that featured skin diver–related stories. Little Johnny hollered at the skin diver, "Hey, I saw you on *Sea Hunt* the other day!"

Another vacation that sticks out in my mind is in the early 1950s, together with the Neets, it was decided that we'd like to go to Canada to enjoy the scenery and camp at different parks along the way. Otis and I each had our ten days of vacation and we wanted to go farther than Vancouver, BC, and on to Banff, Canada. Lake Louise was there and we envisioned a good time as always. And though it was a bit of a drive, we did have a good time as we saw different things. At that time Banff was a neat little Canadian town, located within snowcapped mountains, very English and quaint, quite different from our ocean trips.

Both families traveled to Alberta and the ice fields and saw the glaciers—ice as far as one could see. We then saw Lake Louise; my, was that beautiful! The Lake Louise Hotel was very impressive from the exterior, though we dared not stay there as we couldn't afford it. Fortunately, there were a lot of campsites and the surrounding mountains were just magnificent. We made camp right by the lakeside, though it was a little cold as there was snow still on the mountaintops. And the mosquitoes! There were thousands of them and boy, were they big ones. Mosquito repellent hardly did any good. Poor Patty Kay, Otis and Margie's daughter. The mosquitoes took a liking to her and she was just miserable as she couldn't get away from them. Despite these pests Otis and I went trout fishing in the lake. Now I am not a fisherman, but here the fish were so easy to catch and eager to take the bait. After a short while of this we humorously said that we'd best bait the hook behind a tree so the fish couldn't see it before we cast into the water. Otis and I caught several fish and had enough for a hearty dinner and breakfast as well. Everybody loved the meal.

There was a trail around Lake Louise that provided us opportunities to go for short walks. Once Otis and I went walking while Dick Jr. and Jimmy, our older sons, went running ahead of us. After a short while Dick Jr. and Jimmy came running back with their eyes as big as saucers, screaming that there was a bear on the trail ahead. Otis and I did not take them too seriously, but as we continued to walk, we kept an eye out. Eventually we did come upon this bear. It was huge, probably ten feet tall as it stood up on its hind legs with its front paws in the air. It was a mother brown bear with cubs located nearby in a tree. Needless to say, we immediately turned around and returned to camp.

After a few days at Lake Louise we started back home. It was a pleasant drive and we stopped occasionally along the way. At one pull-out we noticed on one of the mountaintops nearby to Lake Louise there was a sky lift that went to the mountaintop. I remember some discussion of riding this lift, but I don't recall if any of us went up. At another location along a river, we stopped and Otis did some fishing and landed a Dolly Varden, a beautiful fish. Janet, Dick Jr., Sherry Lynn, and Tony were seeking treasures in the riverbed while I lounged by the car. Out of nowhere I spotted a bear by the river not too far from where we were located. I hollered, "You guys better get to the car because there is a bear close by." My family all saw the bear and started screaming and running to the car. I jumped in and locked the door. When everyone reached the car, they attempted to get in but couldn't because brave dad had locked the doors. I continued to yell at them to get in and then finally realized what I had done. Boy, was I embarrassed and did we ever enjoy a laugh over that.

Anyway, our trip was fun except for the mosquitoes and some cold weather. We finally headed for home, feeling that we had a good time and thankful that we were all coming home safe. Arriving home after a vacation was always fun because the family could sleep in our own beds and feel the warmth of our home, anticipating all of the usual and familiar things to be done: the kids would go back to school; I'd return to work that I enjoyed; Janet would continue taking care of Dennis Monroe, Hazel's son; our uncomplicated lives would start up again and all would be back to normal. I can't remember how we handled taking care of Janet's father, Grandpa, when we went on vacation as he lived with us during some of those times. I'm sure it was managed reasonably. My older son Dick Jr. tells me Janet's sister Beverly took care of him.

My Personal Life Choices of Family Consequence

When we returned from this trip to our home at Cycle Lane, two of Janet's younger brothers, Jack and Cal, came to live with us. Though Jack was a young adult, very good hearted, he was a bit slow and perhaps three years behind his peers in maturity. He was family so we took him in. Jack would call Dick Jr., my oldest son, Rocky, and he loved all the kids in the family. Cal, being younger, was finishing high school at Garfield and enjoyed living back with family once again. As I recall, Jack eventually moved out to a rooming house found for him through the welfare office. Cal, who was a hell of a baseball pitcher at Garfield High School, set several records that stood for many years in Seattle's High School Metro League. When he graduated in 1952, I seem to recall that he was sought after by the Chicago Cubs and the Philadelphia Phillies. Cal finally chose to remain in Seattle upon completing negotiation of a very favorable contract with the Seattle Rainiers that same year, playing for them and their farm teams through the mid-fifties prior to being drafted into the army.

Our family lived at Cycle Lane for about four years, continuing to enjoy our next-to-perfect lives, not lacking for too many things, and able to afford the necessities of life. Janet and I were not in a hurry to live a faster life as we were just a normal family like so many others. Perhaps we lacked a more Christian life, which could have been a failing. However, since I was a Catholic thanks to my time with the Mendozas, after we moved from Cycle Lane, Janet and the kids eventually attended catechism and studied to become Catholic as well. The children received their first communions and confirmations when they were old enough, and we all regularly attended mass as a family for several years.

James Harris was now a real estate salesman for a South End Seattle area realty firm; I believe by that time he had sold his used car business. When he would come over to pick up his stepson, Dennis, if I was home at the time, we would visit and he would tell me how well he was doing in his business. He always seemed to have money and drove a new car. At the time I could not have been less interested but James was being friendly and making conversation. This kind of exchange carried on for some time while Janet and I continued to live our predictable, satisfying lifestyle. One day James informed me that he owned a small two-bedroom home in White Center in the Highland Park area. Janet and I had remotely thought about buying a house, especially since the Neets, and our mutual friends the Clarks, had done so and both had moved to the Burien area. And since I was making more money at the time, owning a home seemed like the right thing to do. So one day James came to pick up Dennis and I asked him about the house in White Center. Janet and I eventually bought this 750-square-foot, two-bedroom house with a detached garage. We paid James $7,000 for it and we moved sometime in 1953 to the south Seattle area of White Center located at 9033 11th Avenue SW.

I was still working at City Light and our lifestyle was very satisfying. Our family was growing and Grandpa was living with us, so our lives were well occupied and our financial obligations were few. Upon moving into our new, little home, we filled it up right away with all the family. Grandpa and Dick Jr. had one bedroom, Tony and Sherry had the second one, and Janet and I slept in the living room on a sofa bed. She and I did this for about two or three years until Grandpa moved in 1956 to an old, downtown Seattle Hotel located on Yesler. Nicholas passed away in 1957 at age seventy-five.

This little house gave us some roots. It had a nice backyard with a single car garage accessible from an alleyway, some trees, and a small garden area. The garage had an unfinished room, which I continued to work at completing. Eventually, we did get some use out of the room once finished, when Janet's younger brother Cal went into the army and was shipped overseas. He had his young wife, Connie, stay for a short while in this finished room. We had a corner grocery store one block away and it was two blocks to Highland Park Elementary School. As always Janet made some good friends with our new neighbors, and she continued to make the family a wonderful, normal home with no dreams of grandeur.

Sometime around 1954 or 1955, Janet's taking care of Dennis Monroe came to an unexpected and tragic end. Dennis, who was around fourteen years old at the time, and a very intellectual young man, committed suicide in the family garage while his parents were out for the evening. It was a terrible shock and very unsettling because we had all gotten to know him so well and the whole family liked him. We all had a difficult time understanding why such a young person with so much potential could take his own life. Janet and I offered our sincere support and sympathy to both James and Hazel. It took some time for our family to adjust to this loss as we considered Dennis a part of it.

As the years passed by in our little house, our family and work life continued to be quite comfortable, though James kept after me to consider selling real estate. According to him, making money was easy to do in that business. Well, eventually I succumbed to his encouragement and decided to make a change. That was about 1957. Janet and I talked about it and she went along with me as we could both see the possibilities of making a better life. Little did I know that forty-one years later I would honestly say that was mistake number one! A life choice that would alter—in numerous, measurable, and lasting ways—the course of our family life and our individual lives yet to come.

At the time, had James been a little more forthright with me about the difficulties of making such a change, I believe I would not have done so. I was only thinking positively and there were many things that were negative, but I didn't know about them until I was confronted by them. Mainly, there was no steady income and no benefits, something that I had for many years with Seattle City Light. I had $1,800 from my retirement fund and that was it. But when I decided to make the change, I didn't think I was doing anything wrong, so on the strength of that, it was an OK move.

So I took the plunge. In retrospect, I can't believe that I made such a move so fast. I drew my money out of my retirement account and that would be the funds that would carry us until I sold something. I made one mistake on top of another, not in my business venture but in the way I went about it. I had to take a state real estate exam, which I could not pass at the time as I didn't know enough about the business. So I had to study and James did help me some in that effort, but I was old enough to make my own decisions. Hopefully I had made the right one. First thing, I bought a 1955 Ford because I needed business transportation. I also required a new wardrobe, including suits, shirts, ties, and shoes, in order to look prosperous. And now I had a job that did not pay a steady income. But I was lucky and was a people person. I sold four homes in the first month. Unfortunately, they were all new homes that had to be built and, therefore, I would not see a dime from these sales for about four to five months.

Understanding this new business and how to perform different work-related tasks wasn't easy for me. I had to learn market areas, house styles and types, and other numerous details about houses—oh so many things while I had to prepare for the state exam. The other major mistake I made was that I could have gone back to City Light within thirty days of my departure. Tough to reflect on mistakes, especially when other people judge you on them. So I just didn't go back. I went to real estate school and passed the exam and life went on, not an easy life though. This was mainly because of the personal financial struggles, which are inherent in the real estate business, establishing a future pattern for me and my family. I always had sales that would close but they took time, and in the meantime, there were bills to pay, kids to feed, and shoes to buy. So Seattle First National Bank controlled my life from then on.

Anyway, because our lives were changing seemingly for the better, we started thinking about another home, maybe larger. At that time in 1958, a builder, Lloyd Ferrell, was going to construct some homes in a project called Burien Hills, just northeast of Burien. These homes were large, with three bedrooms, a double carport, a living room with fireplace, a dining room, a kitchen, a single bath, a full unfinished basement with fireplace, sundeck and a wooded lot—all for $16,500. Janet and I discussed it and decided that we certainly needed more room, especially with two teenagers and Tony soon to be. By that time it was just our family then as Grandpa had passed away and Janet's younger sister and brothers had all gone on with their separate lives.

The family was ready for a nicer home and was excited to be stepping up. Our little house went up for sale even though the new home was not yet under construction. We were impatient! At that time construction of a new home would take three to four months to complete. Our little house quickly sold, so we moved into a small rental house just north of the airport in the Boulevard

Park area at 128th and 23rd Avenue South. We didn't pay much rent but were so excited about our new home as it never occurred to us that we would be able to afford such a new house. I continued at my new job, doing OK, making more money, though not noticeable. I applied for a GI loan, which was approved, and we financed this new home just fine. In time the house was finished. Janet had picked out the carpet and other interior finishes and appliances throughout the house so that every room reflected her choices. It was a beautiful home that sat on a large wooded lot overlooking the north runways of Seattle-Tacoma Airport, with a Mount Rainier view in the background and a big sundeck off the dining room with stairs down to the yard. This was before jet travel and the airport was a lot smaller with fewer flights. While we lived there, though, our family bore witness to the birth of jet travel in its early years.

When it came time to move, all of our kids had to go to different schools. Sherry Lynn went to Puget Sound Junior High School, Tony went down the hill to a brand-new school, Sunny Terrace Elementary, and Dick Jr. went to Highline High School for his sophomore year, later transferring to the recently completed Glacier High School because our new home was located in that new high school's district. Janet's and my world was full of life and excitement. Of course, our home had to have all new furniture, which was the beginning of our getting into debt. From then on it was easy, nothing to it, a piece of cake. But the bank was always there and I was always at the bank, easy come, easy go.

My personal life became a little more complicated as I had too much time and I enjoyed it. Our house was still home base, but my behavior became less responsible as I was confronted with opportunities and freedoms that came with the new territory in which I found myself. I no longer led a blue-collar life but slowly transitioned to 1960s white-collar business realities and lifestyles. Somehow the money became a merry-go-round. We were living quite well, certainly beyond our means. I would go to the bank to borrow and go to pay when a deal closed, and I continued our deficit-financing lifestyle. What a false illusion of prosperity it was!

The home remained our main focus. To maintain a family life, I finished off the basement rec room first, and then shortly afterward, the bathroom and bedroom areas for Tony who was now a teenager. Actually, Janet and I worked together to accomplish this project and we had fun doing it. During this time the family enjoyed some vacations to California. We always drove because it was fun as we always had new cars to drive and I had relatives in San Diego and San Jose, California, as well as Mexicali and Calexico, Mexico.

Somehow the business life became more complicated in those years. Alcohol was a main part of business activity then and drinking parties always seemed to be a part of the landscape. Banks, mortgage, escrow and realty companies, the builders—man, it never ended; drinking was a major pastime structured to enlist and secure business deals. I wasn't much of a drinker but I was learning. Fortunately, my family never saw me drunk as I had much respect for them and I knew that drinking could really mess one's life up. But my personal life was changing. Our camping trips with the Neets became fewer to nonexistent. I was working too many hours, less time off, spending too much money on material things, and that never stopped until Janet and I were forced to make some lifestyle adjustments.

Finally we had to sell our pride and joy, our new home, in order to clear the many bills that had been accumulated. We were able to find a real nice house in the Normandy Vista area just south of Burien off of First Avenue and South 197th Street. So in 1962 we moved. It was not a new home but it was homey. This move disrupted the kids again, especially Sherry Lynn, as she was planning on becoming a cheerleader at Glacier High School and now she had to transfer to Highline High School. This was a most traumatic change for her. She took it real hard as she had her heart set on being a cheerleader and she was very good at it. So many times things happen in life that are so different to your experience that it totally changes your life. In this instance, Sherry Lynn lost all further interest in becoming a cheerleader or participating in that activity at Highline High School. Tony had to leave his peer group friends once again, but he seemed to adapt to the change quite well, taking it in stride and adjusting accordingly. Dick Jr. had graduated from high school by that time, so the move did not particularly affect him. This move later proved the harbinger of further changes to come to our family; it was only the tip of the iceberg.

As business went, I was doing OK, able to take care of our obligations, but I was working longer hours, spending less time at home, and when I was home, my mind and heart were not there. One year led to the next and so I put on a false pretense that everything was OK, but I was only fooling myself. I just didn't have the guts to admit that I was no longer happy in my marriage even though I tried to imagine that I was. Deep down inside I was so sad because I knew I was hurting my family, but I felt helpless to help myself and to do what was right. So I kept pretending that things would work out and be OK, knowing full well that my marriage was not OK and that more bad truths were to unfold in our family life and reveal themselves.

I can never say that my wife, Janet, didn't understand what was happening between us. She was most understanding throughout this uncoupling process. To this day I feel deep remorse and pain in my heart for what I did to my family and my wife, and my heart still is hurting. After several years of my personal inability or refusal to listen to my heart and correct the course of my life back to my family, Janet and I finally divorced in 1975 after thirty-three years of marriage.

Tears come to my eyes when I think back because things have changed so much over the past forty-five years. Janet and I have been divorced for twenty-two years; I have been remarried for just about as long; Otis has passed away; my daughter, Sherry Lynn, is also deceased, as is her childhood friend Patty Kay, Otis and Margie's daughter, both from cancer; and all of our individual lives have changed as our other children have grown and taken their places among the baby-boom generation. I am now seventy-six years old and Janet is seventy-three. And as I reflect on the past, so many more memories come to mind and stand out as fun and happy moments in time, as well as significant crossroads that altered the course of our family experience and tore us from one another.

This is an account herein of my lifetime of fifty-three years from birth in 1922 to the end of my marriage to Janet in 1975. Life was not fair sometimes during my early years. And in my earlier adult life, on occasion, my character was not strong, knowledgeable, or experienced enough to handle the scope of new realities confronting me. Times changed as I was living them. The crazy sixties and seventies influenced a lot of my life experiences then. The temptations, influences, the availability of money, the lack of never having had a more formal education nor single life before getting married so young, always having had a serious outlook about personal responsibilities, and the so-called need of doing something for oneself, all seemed to have played a role in my personal confusion and uncoupling from my marriage and family. My second life, the following twenty-two years to date, has certainly been different from my first. But the one remaining fact is that my mind is full of old memories and an aching heart sometimes never heals. May the good Lord forgive me for all the wrongs that I have done. I dedicate my personal story to my two sons, Dick Jr. and Tony, and my deceased daughter, Sherry Lynn. God bless them.

My Personal Life Choices of Family Consequence

Calvin Humphreys, eighteen years old, noted Garfield High School pitcher. He was a three-sports athlete letterman. After being drafted by the Seattle Rainiers, Cal pitched for them in the mid-1950s, including during Fred Hutchinson's time as skipper of the club. Family photo album.

Two for You, One for Me

This is an Assessor's Office photograph of our first family house, all 750 square feet of it: two bedrooms, one bath, living room, small kitchen with eating area, and heating by an oil-burning furnace that was lit with a match and burning newspaper. There was an undeveloped, dirt alley in back of the detached garage you see behind the house that served all homes on the block on both alley sides. Our garage had space for one vehicle, a workbench area and a second-story storage area accessible by wall ladder, coupled with an extra floor-level room that my father eventually finished into another bedroom. The house and garage look similar today. Courtesy of Puget Sound Regional Archives, Washington State.

Department of Assessments 1958 photo. Needless to say this home was quite a step up for our family and a major transition from blue-collar surroundings to the new and emerging post-WWII middle class. This house looks similar today with the exception of an added shed within the carport area. In a recent drive-by I discovered remains of the collapsed, painted fence that my dad and I built together to separate the north property line from the street and shoulder. No one was home at the house, so I plan on dropping by in the near future to barter for a piece of that fence! Courtesy of Puget Sound Regional Archives, Washington State.

Two for You, One for Me

The Normandy Vista house in which we resided as a whole family until my parents divorced. My mother lived in this home for a period of time before moving on with her life for several years as a single woman before marrying a second time. Of course by that time my siblings and I had all gone off to start our adult lives, my brother as a journeyman electrician, my sister as a stewardess for Western Airlines, and I continued my undergraduate and postgraduate college education. This home, though a different color, still looks the same. Family album photo.

HERNANDEZ FAMILY MEMORIES

Cycle Lane entrance through the kitchen, my mom, Janet, and me, Tony, age four. All following images are from family photo collections.

Two for You, One for Me

My sister, Sherry Lynn, age about four, on her tricycle I believe in front of the Lanham duplex where we previously lived.

My dad, Richard, with his children, Sherry Lynn, Tony, and Dick Jr. at the High Point Projects, West Seattle, about 1951 or 1952.

My Personal Life Choices of Family Consequence

Uncle Cal with brother Dick Jr., "Rocky" as his uncles all called him, and Uncle Jack with Tony, Cycle Lane duplex.

Richard and Janet, 1956, in front of our first house that we owned in White Center. Dad had transitioned from Seattle City Light to real estate agent.

Two for You, One for Me

My sister Sherry Lynn's First Communion.

Dick Jr. and Tony about 1955.

My Personal Life Choices of Family Consequence

My parents, Janet and Richard, walking on the Washington State Ferry going from Anacortes up to Orcas Island and then San Juan Island. During the 1950s Washington State ferries were much smaller and carried significantly LESS cars than they do now. The following photos, except one from Orcas Island, are from San Juan County Park, and all photo frames were taken from family 8-mm camera film.

Our campsite with the Neet family. This campground now has established campsites and nicely constructed bathroom facilities and shared water source, and FEES. In our time we camped where we chose, and provided our own portable toilet with privacy blanket and handily dug waste hole, thanks to Dad and Otis. I recall that there was limited water availability, little or no fees, and the park was never crowded but with rabbits. What still remains, however, is the old, but still standing, small, two-story pioneer home adjacent to the circulation drive just south of the now available bathroom facilities, and the Ranger Check-in log facility. Hopefully the County Park rehabs both landmarks so they remain another one hundred years.

In the above photo, Otis Neet on the left, and his son, Jimmy, on the right, cooking the rabbit BBQ feast. The Neets were our immediate duplex neighbors at Cycle Lane and our families continued this annual camping fun for several years over the holidays and school summer vacations.

At last we get to feast on rabbit! Otis Neet standing, Margie, Patty Kay, and Jimmy sitting on the left of the table, with my dad and I sitting on the right side, with one of my siblings in between us, don't know who; I'm sure Mom was operating the movie camera.

My Personal Life Choices of Family Consequence

*My brother Richard Jr. sitting on the right tractor seat, and me sitting behind the wheel, and Jimmy Neet on the vehicle far left in the photo with just his head showing, all imagining what fun it would be to get the opportunity to net rabbits rather than shooting them.
Note the net at the front of the vehicle.*

Most likely Dick Jr.'s cake to celebrate his birthday on our annual July trips to the San Juans. Janet, Tony, Sherry Lynn, Patty Kay, and Margie in the striped shirt. Looks like I sure am liking that cake!

All the kids on the raft: Dick Jr. in the center, Tony in front of him, Jimmy on my right with his hands on the pole, Patty Kay on the far left, with Sherry Lynn behind our brother. I wonder if kids still do this kind of stuff? I hope so!

My Personal Life Choices of Family Consequence

Sherry Lynn and Patty Kay playing with their dolls. Look Mom, no cell phone!

Janet and Margie taking it easy with the Neet's youngest family member Johnny, age three or four. One day the ladies walked way up the mountainside just opposite the camp to the east and my dad was actually able to view them in the camera and took some footage of them waving from the top at all of us. Our families always enjoyed viewing the moms on film doing this, as at the time, we all didn't think that these "old" gals had it in them.

This image always got a laugh when the families gathered to watch camping movies. This particular shot was from Orcas Island Moran State Park; Margie and Janet doing "ladies" laundry in large dish pans. The colored shot of this is certainly more risqué!

Photo taken on the island's west side road scenic drive after leaving the County Park on the way to Friday Harbor to probably get groceries, other essentials, or just take a lovely drive to sightsee with Otis and Margie.

SON'S EPILOGUE

In bringing my father's story to a close, I feel an obligation to the reader to leave you with knowing that my father remarried in the 1970s to a lovely woman named Joan. Their marriage lasted about thirty-three years until his passing on June 6, 2012. Of course, this second marriage was different from that which brought about and created a new life and direction in my father's early years with my mother. His second marriage took him in other directions with other opportunities and experiences that only added to his total life experience in new, different, and meaningful ways. For me, as a single man earlier in Dad and Joan's marriage and later on as a married man myself, our families made many warm memories of holidays, celebrations, and spending quality time together, doing shared activities whenever possible. Thankfully, both my brother and sister and their loved ones were, earlier on, part of these experiences as well.

It is interesting to note that my father finally left the real estate business after nineteen eventful and life-altering years. Believe it or not, he returned to Seattle City Light during the late 1970s and they welcomed him back with open arms, even crediting toward his retirement the earlier years he spent working there. In fact, there were still people working at City Light that remembered him from the previous employment. He retired from City Light in the 1990s after working for several years in the safety division of Seattle City Light.

My father had an incredible life with many of its extremes of tough times and joy. Dad's life was out of his control in his formative early years, but later he was also blessed with life-changing people, many new and wonderful experiences, satisfactions, a loving family and friends, some successes, and, yes, shortcomings and failures. But, by God, he made a life for himself from pretty much nothing in the beginning. From my personal perspective my father's life overall was well lived in many respects, and far surpassed his difficult, challenging beginning, and the slipping away from the loving home life he and my mother created for themselves and their children. In my total being, his love and laughter will always ring in my heart, and hopefully, on occasion I will continue to hear his whistle!

I want to share with the reader why this story was brought to an end in the manner that it was by my dad. In my effort to complete this manuscript, I happened upon a note to me from him that was tucked into a large envelope that contained about half of his original handwritten draft. Upon finding and reading his note to me, I was confused in that I did not recall having previously seen it, and if I had, I must have completely forgotten it existed, or had thought at the time that I would remember it when it was needed. Well, sadly I did not remember, but boy, was I happy when I found it!

As background, Dad's writing effort progressed over several years. I don't recall him ever mentioning to me his technique of using a cassette recorder to "make conversation with himself and his emotions." So when I found the above mentioned note, I was elated with the information regarding his nine microcassettes as this seemed to be new information to assist me in my writing on his behalf. I was excited to sit down and listen to these tapes to determine if any of his thoughts were of a substantive nature that could be used to add to, expand on, or clarify any memoir section other than what Dad had actually written down for me. It turned out to be worth the effort!

In respect for my dad's commitment to me to accomplish his personal history of a little over half of his life, I thought it appropriate to use his original note to me to provide the reader with my father's personal handwritten statement of his feelings for bringing the narrative to a conclusion in the manner that he chose. For the benefit of the reader, my dad's unedited, typewritten note follows below, with his original, handwritten version afterward. So with that background, Dad, show off your handwriting:

Tony:

I have gone as far as with this as my will, will let me. The end represents too many aches and hurts. I am glad that to the point of where I finished may be about the things that you wanted to know the rest is history. The tapes that I used to do this are all intact there's nine in number. There is a lot of filler stuff in them as I was making conversation with myself and my emotions. It's taken me several years to do this but it wasn't easy trying to relive almost 70 years of life is just a little bit much. But bottom line I am glad I was able to put some of my life down.

Love Dad

These tapes are my life after 1941

Two for You, One for Me

> Tony:
>
> I've gone as far as with this as my
> will, will let me. The end represents
> to many aches and hurts, I'm glad that to
> the point of where I finished maybe
> about things that you wanted to know
> the rest is history. The tapes that I used
> to do this are all intact there nine in
> number. There is a lot of fuller stuff
> in there as I was making conversation
> with my self and my emotions.
> It taken me several years to do this but
> it was't easy trying to relive almost
> 70 years of life is just a little bit much.
> But bottom line I'm glad I was
> able to put some of my life down.
>
>   Love Dad
>
> These tapes are my life
> after 1941

Dad's closing note to me.

Son's Epilogue

Three generations of Hernández family: Richard Sr. on the right, my son Mark in the middle, and I am on the left. This photo was taken in the early 1990s after my son and I reconnected after not seeing each other since he was born in 1965. My girlfriend at the time and I were in high school and made the difficult choice of giving our child and ourselves the best opportunity for a good life. We made a painful, correct decision, that now all involved are thankful for and grateful for the blessings in life that reconnected my son with both of his biological parents and grandparents. Mark was adopted by two wonderful people and their children, and was raised to become an exceptional man and person. I was able to finish high school and get my undergraduate BA Degree in Business from Central Washington, and a Master's Degree in Health Care Administration from the University of Washington. My ex-girlfriend, Jun, graduated from high school, then moved to another part of the country and started a new life, eventually having a family and returning to the Northwest; she currently continues to have a very successful career. She and I have a good relationship now and are both so proud of our son Mark's life choices, having a wonderful wife, Melissa, and three bright and capable children (our grandkids) and successful career. Personal family photo album.

Two for You, One for Me

Richard E. Hernandez
(August 27, 1922-June 6, 2012)

*A
Service of
Committal
August 27, 2012*

*St. Elizabeth Episcopal Church
1005 SW 152nd Street
P.O. Box 66579 (Mail)
Burien, Washington 98166*

Memorial service remembrance cover.

ABOUT THE AUTHOR

Photograph courtesy of MattLeitholt.com

Anthony Hernández is a first time commercially published author after several years of collaborative effort with his father, Richard Hernández, in bringing his father's memoir to the reading public. As background, in Anthony's health care facilities development career, extensive writing and speaking in both private and public work environments was an integral part of his career. Working through and with a variety of specialized disciplines and professionals, one could say that Anthony made a career of getting decision makers to say yes so that a variety of health care and senior living care centers could be built and services provided to different communities throughout the northwest. Anthony resides with his wife Patty and Frank the cat in the City of Bothell in Washington State, filling their lives with reading, fly fishing, cooking, dining, putting 1000-piece puzzles together, and continuing to set and achieve new life goals.

www.ingramcontent.com/pod-product-compliance
Lightning Source LLC
Chambersburg PA
CBHW061744070526
44585CB00025B/2798